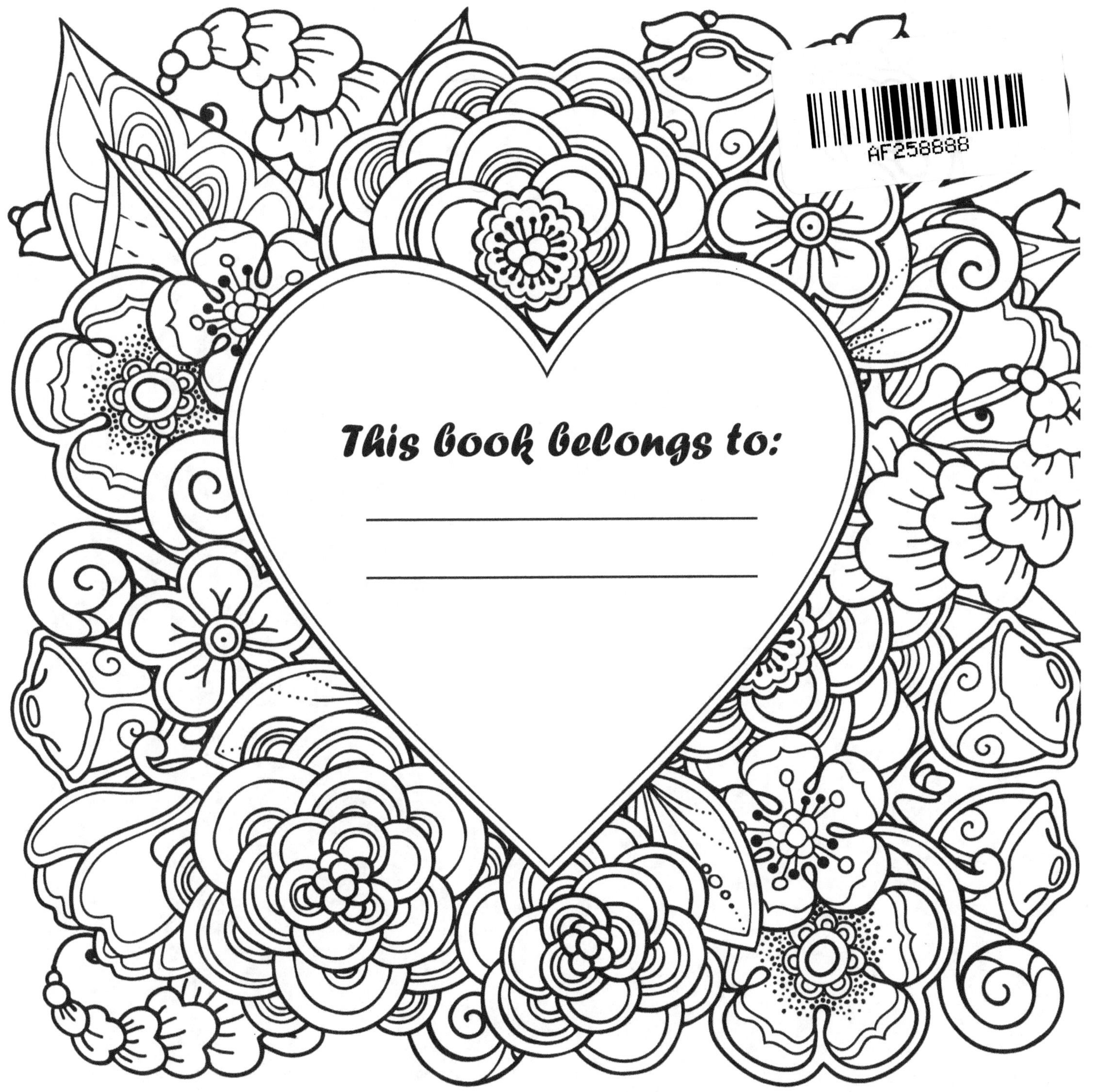

This book belongs to:

Love Mandalas

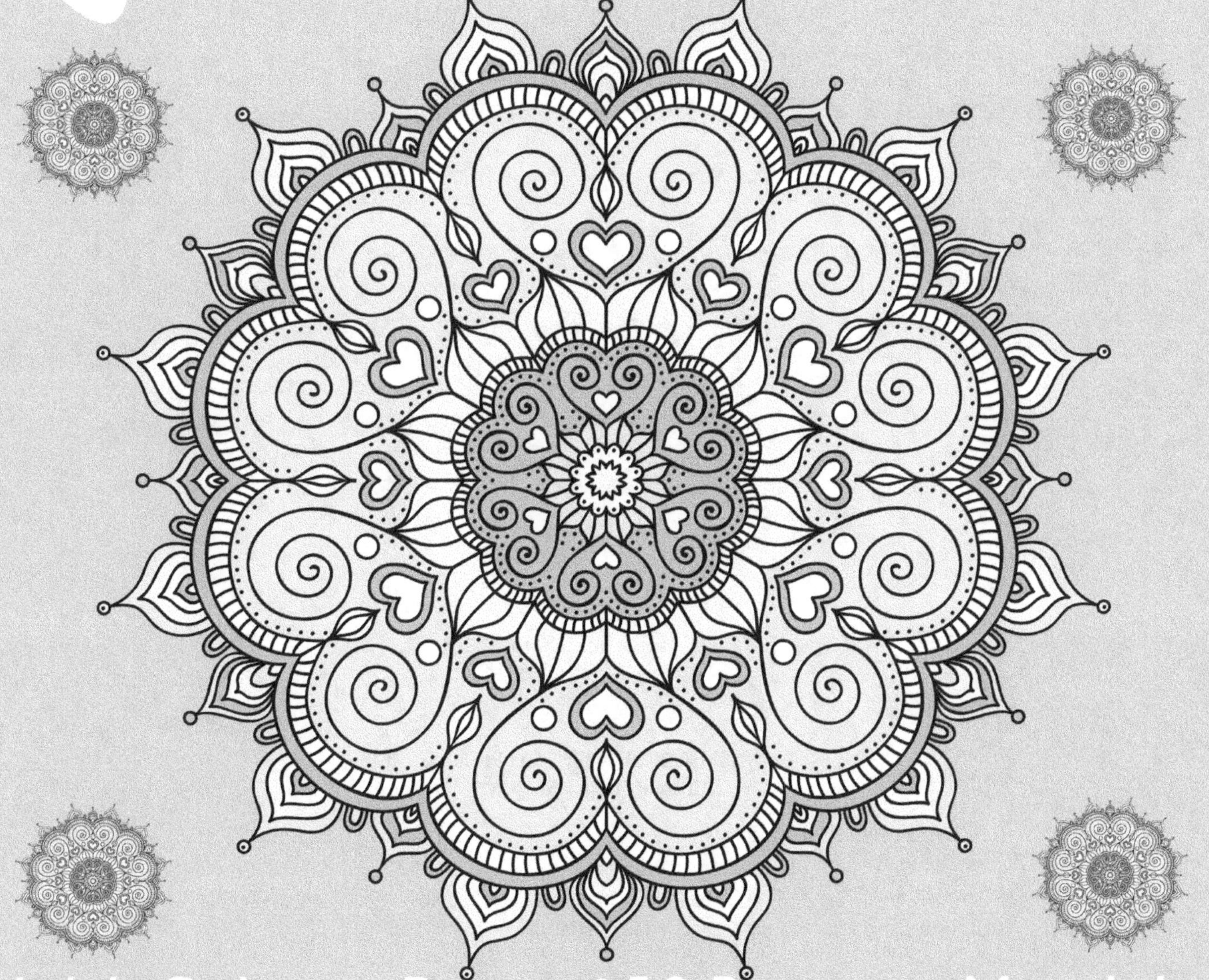

Adult Coloring Book of 50 Romantic Mandalas

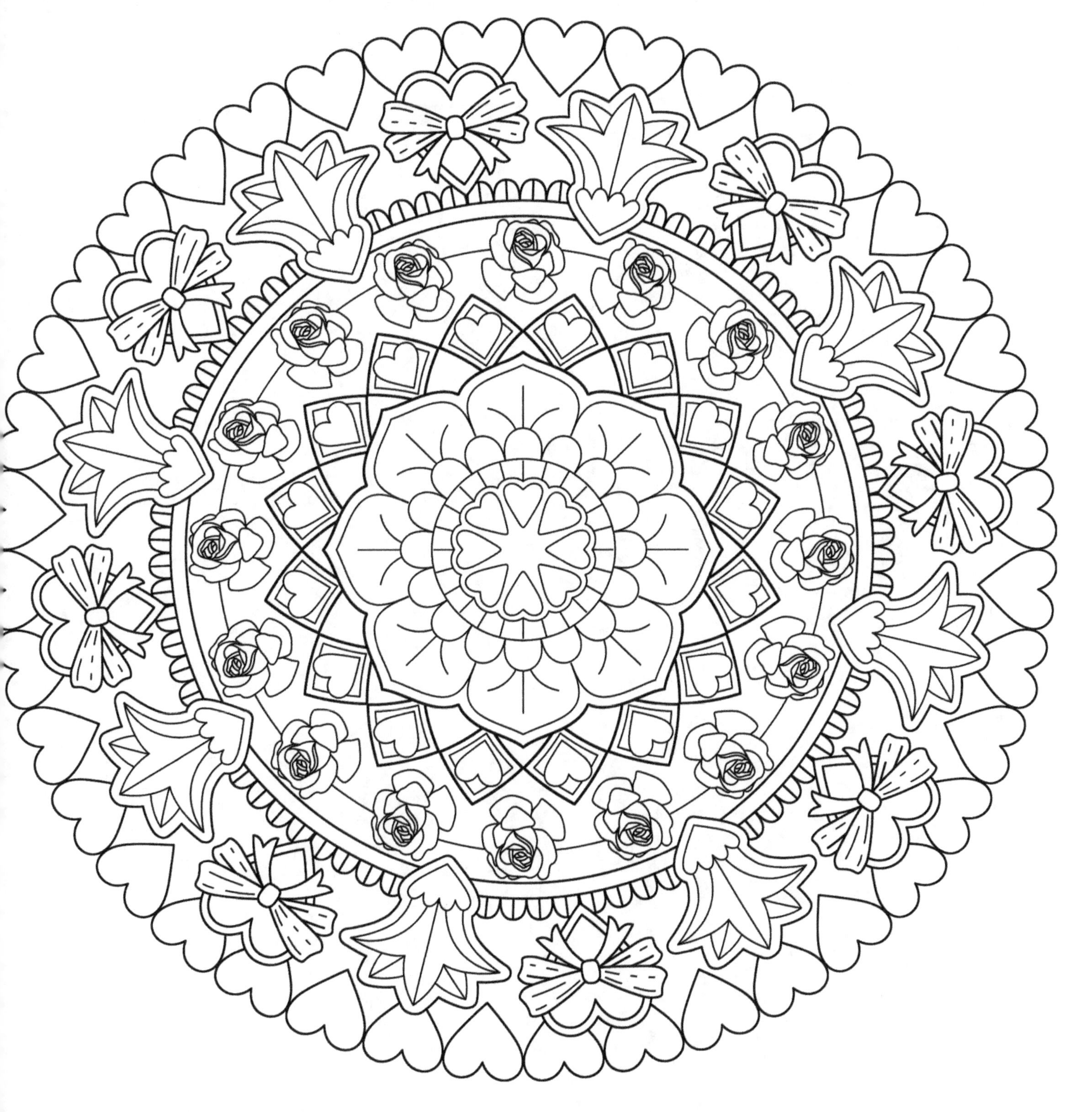

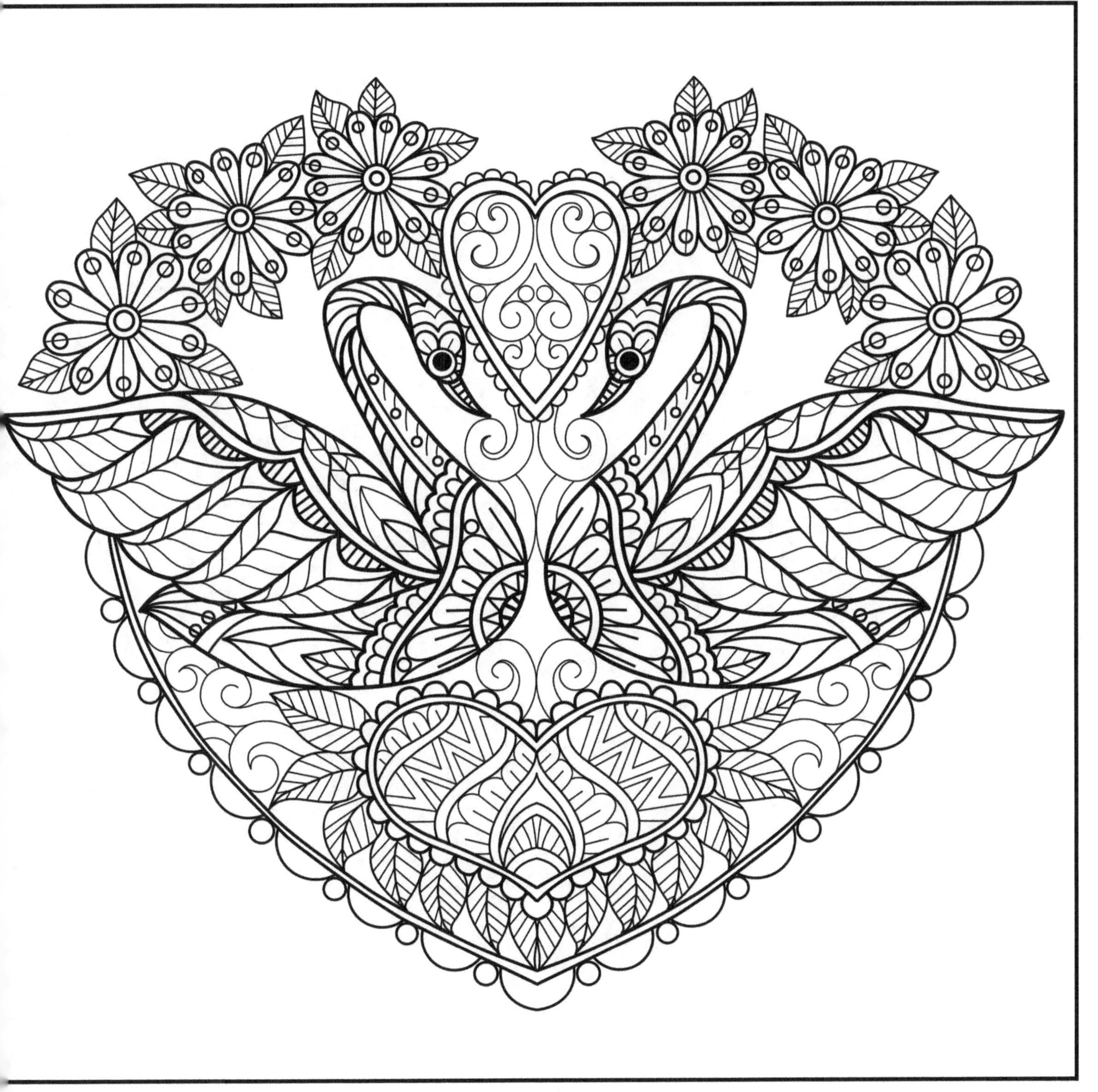

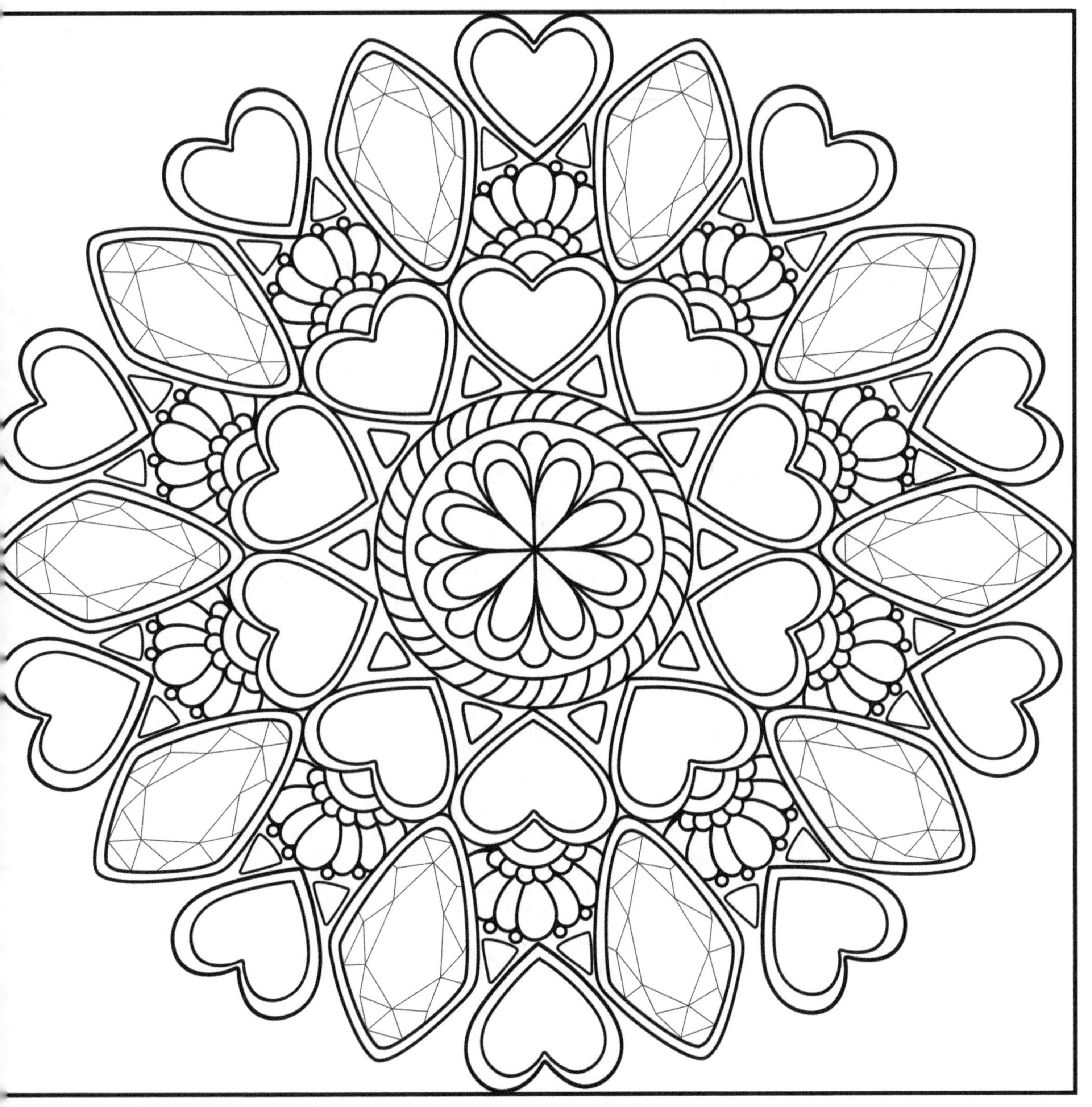

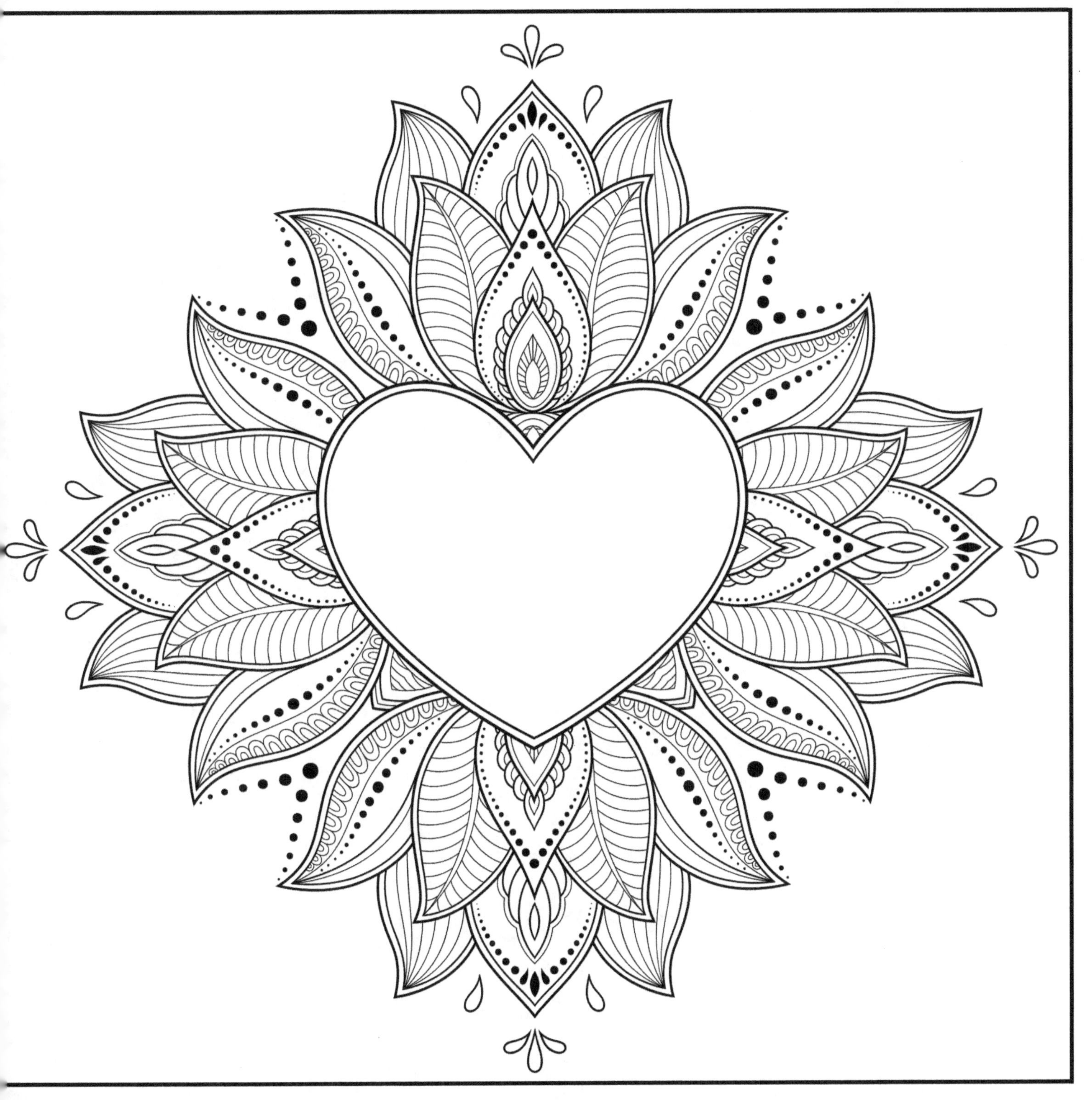

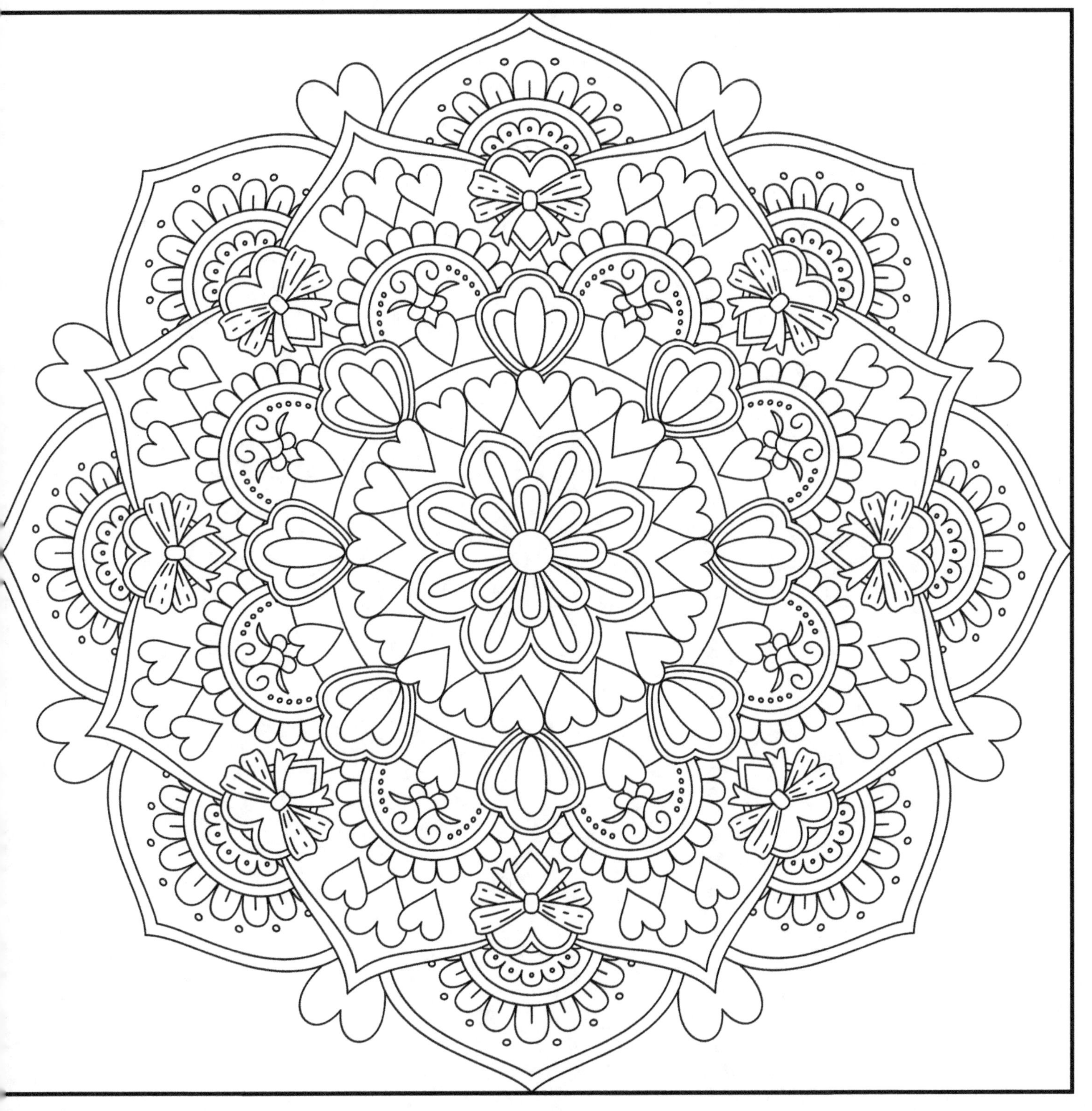

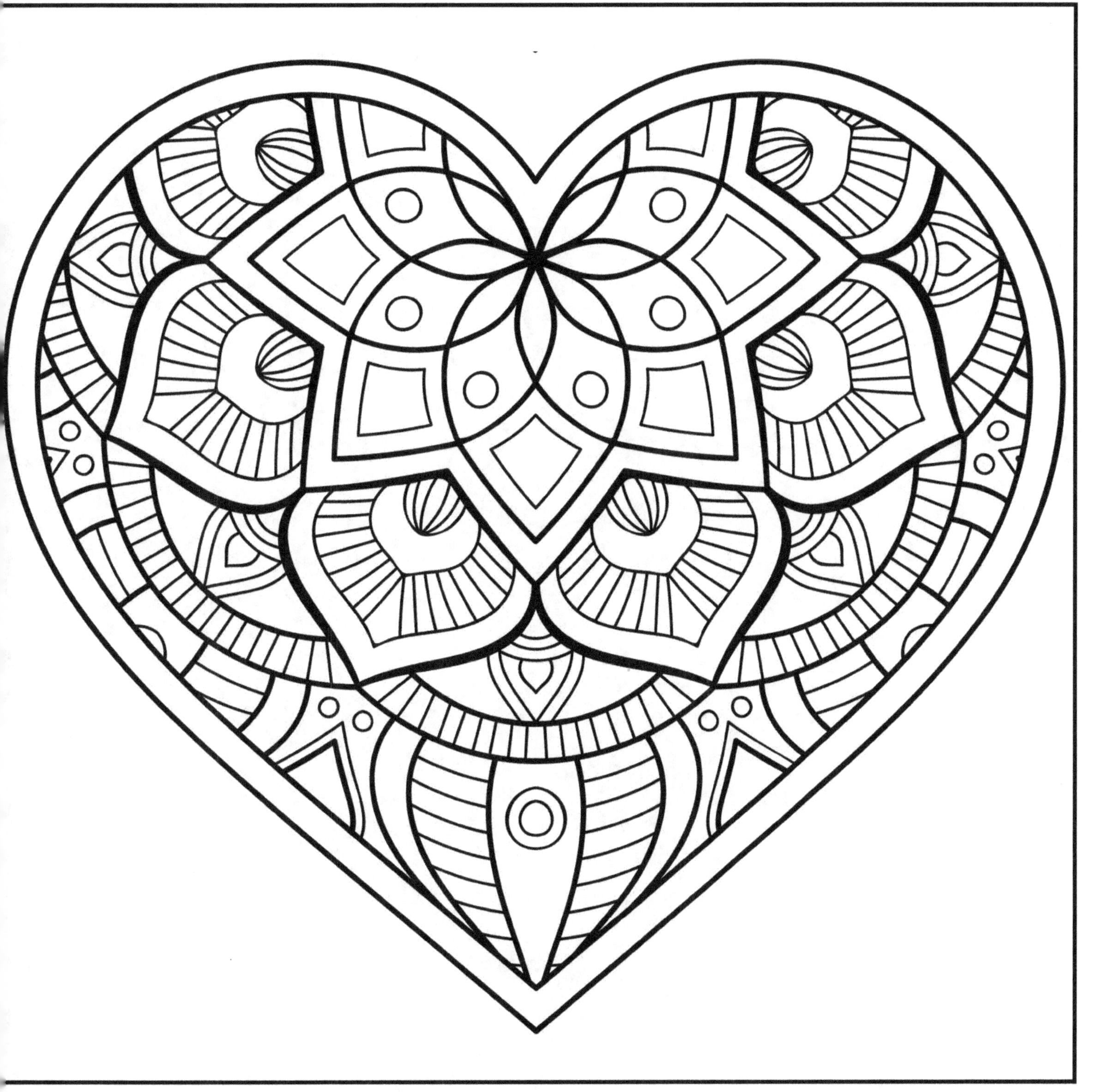

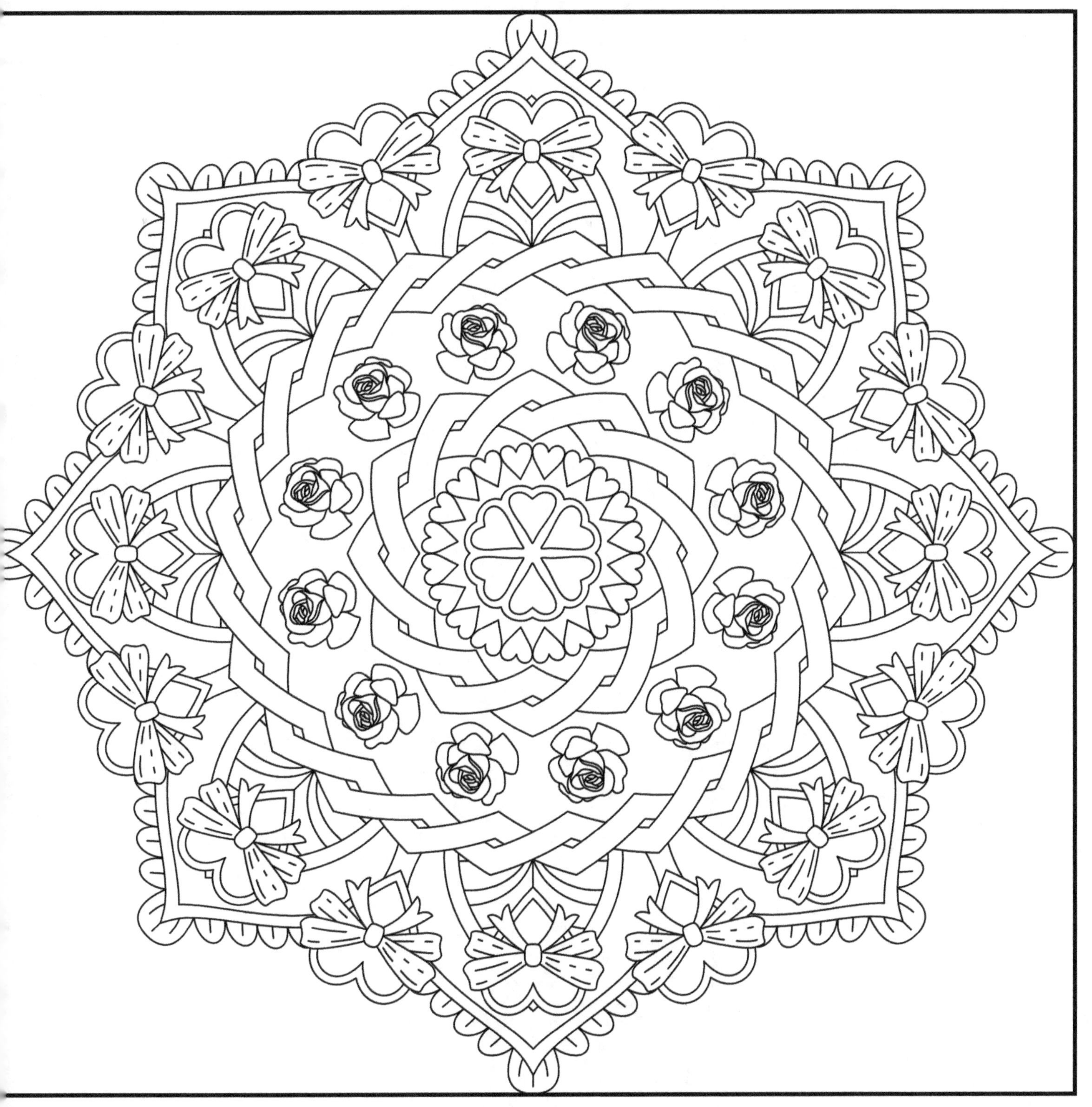

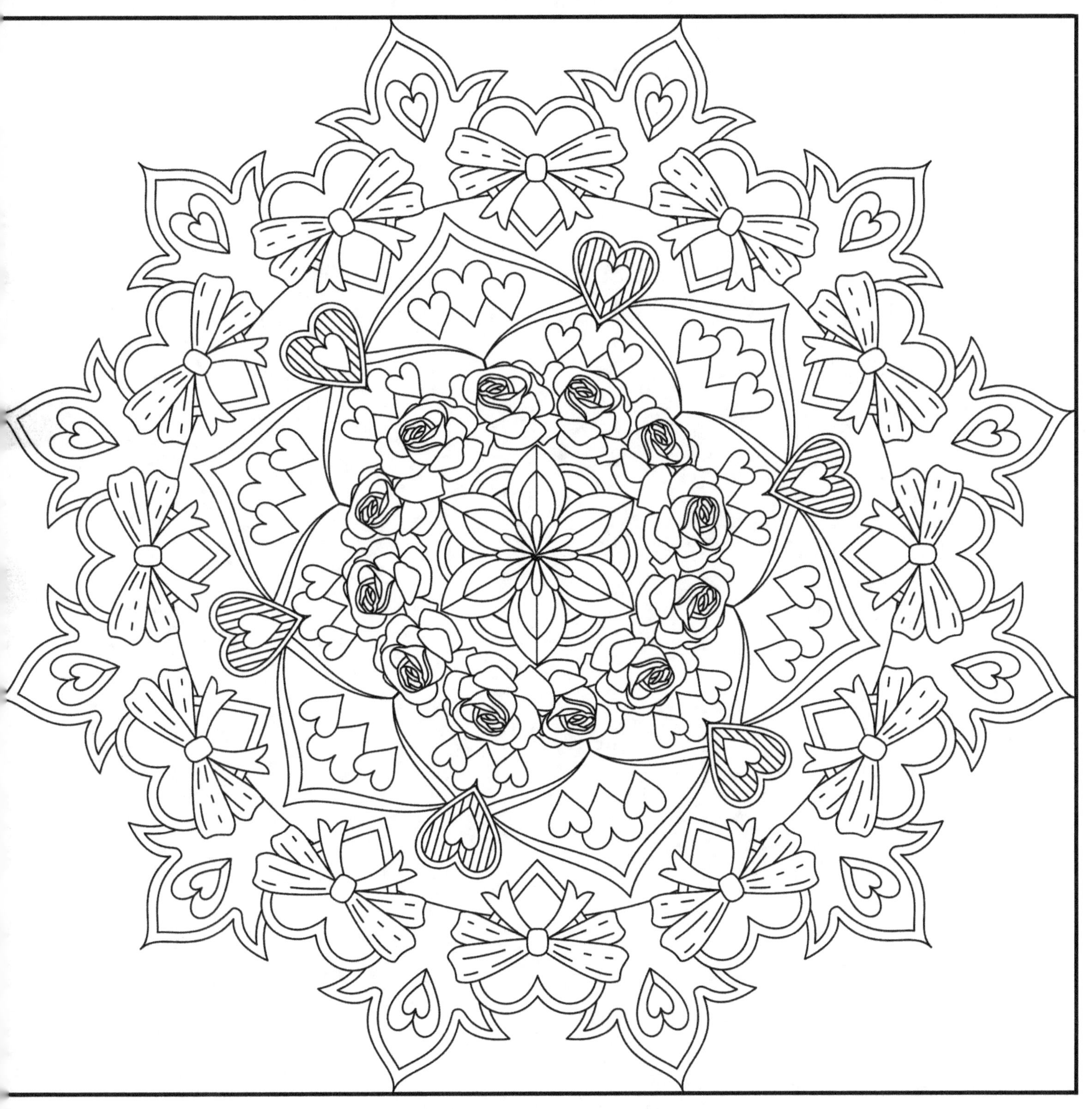

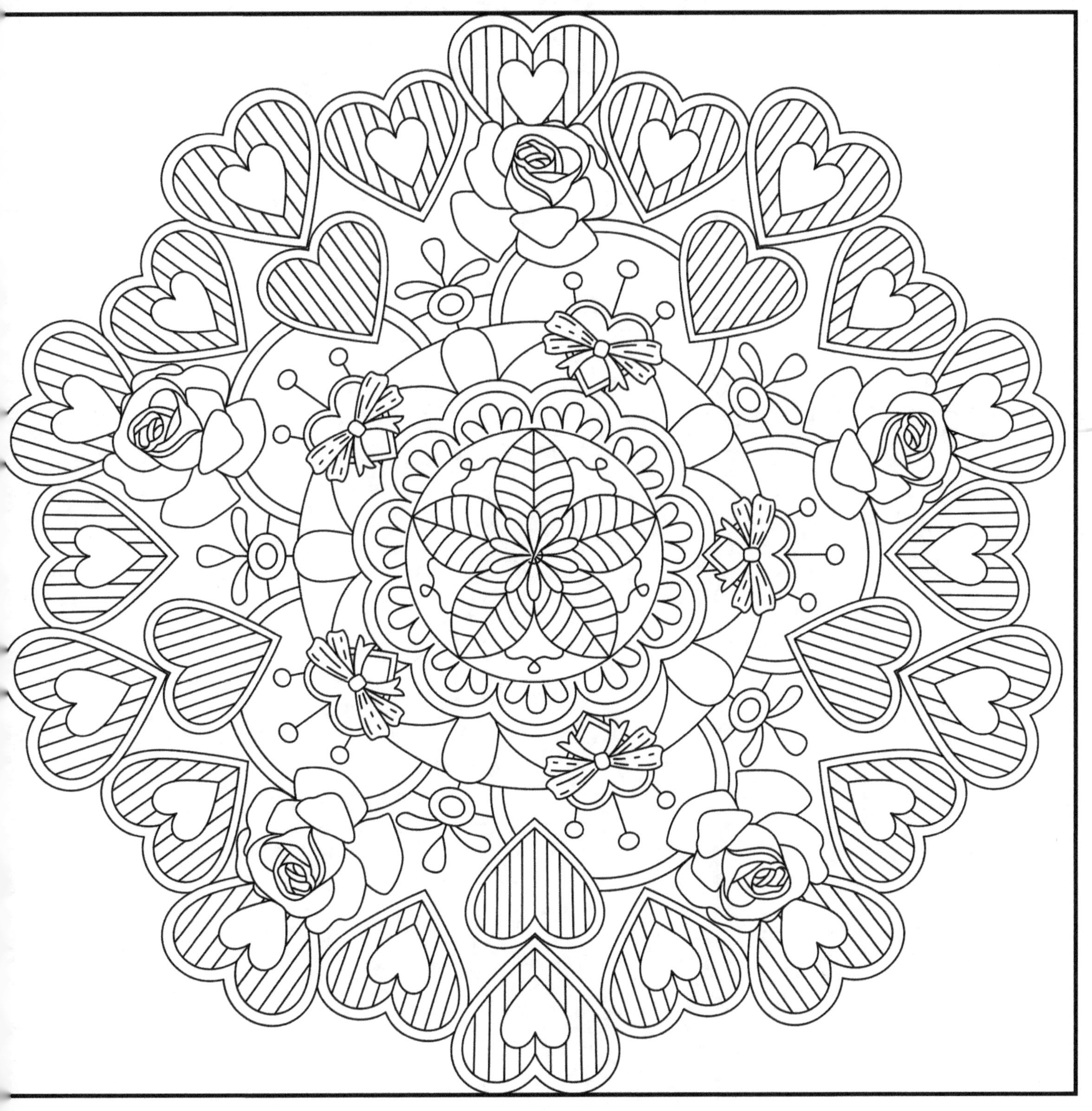

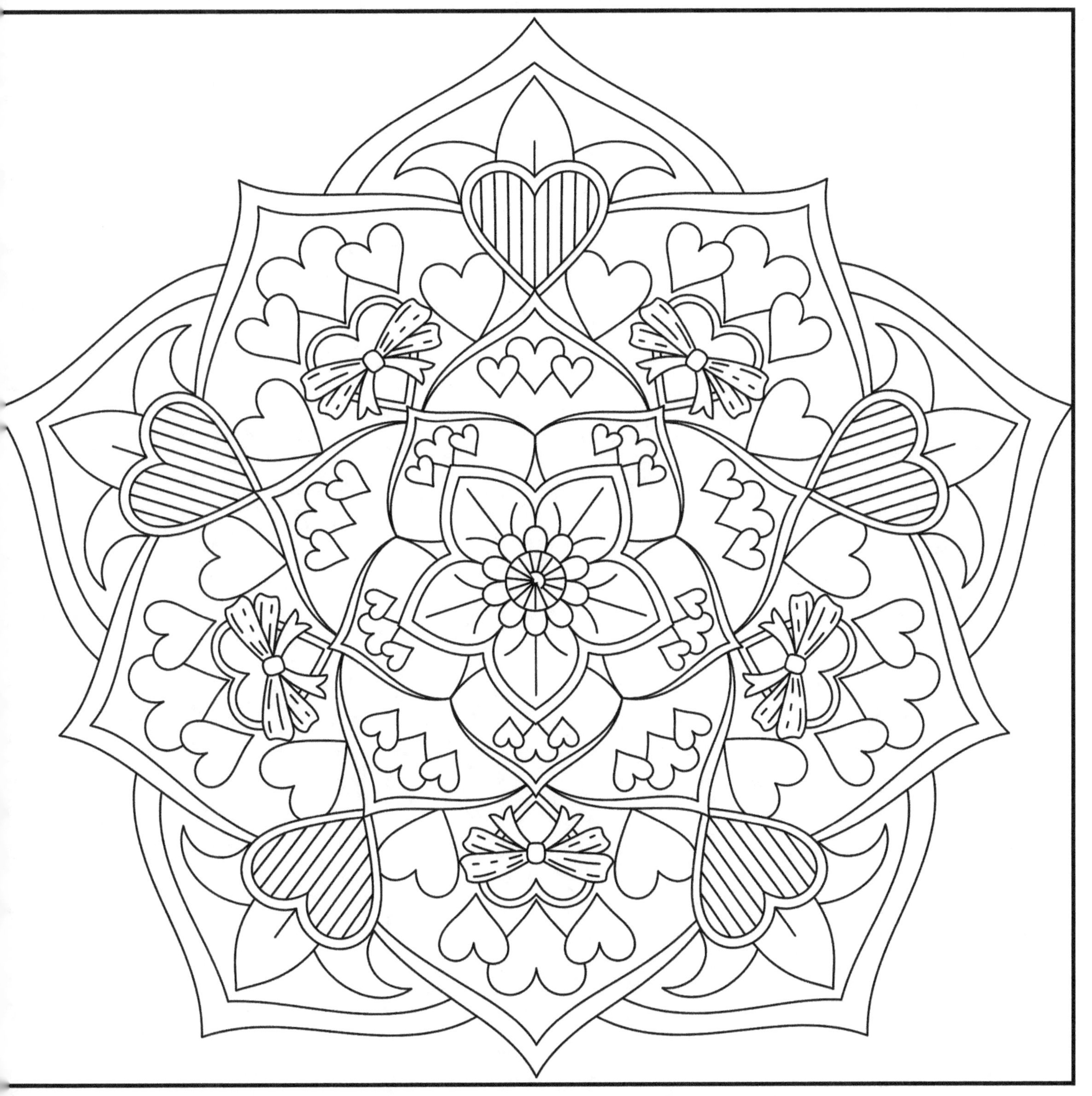

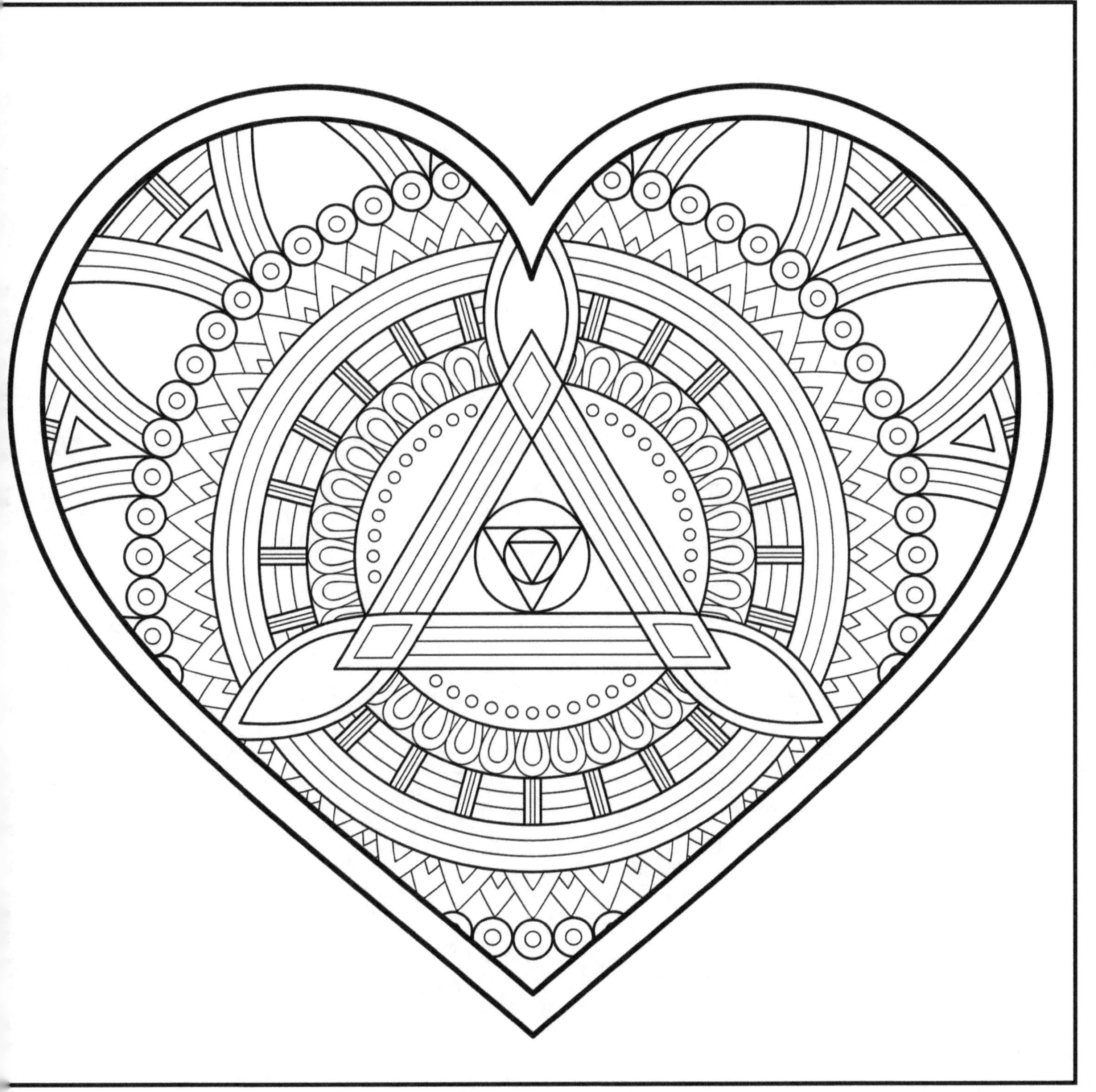

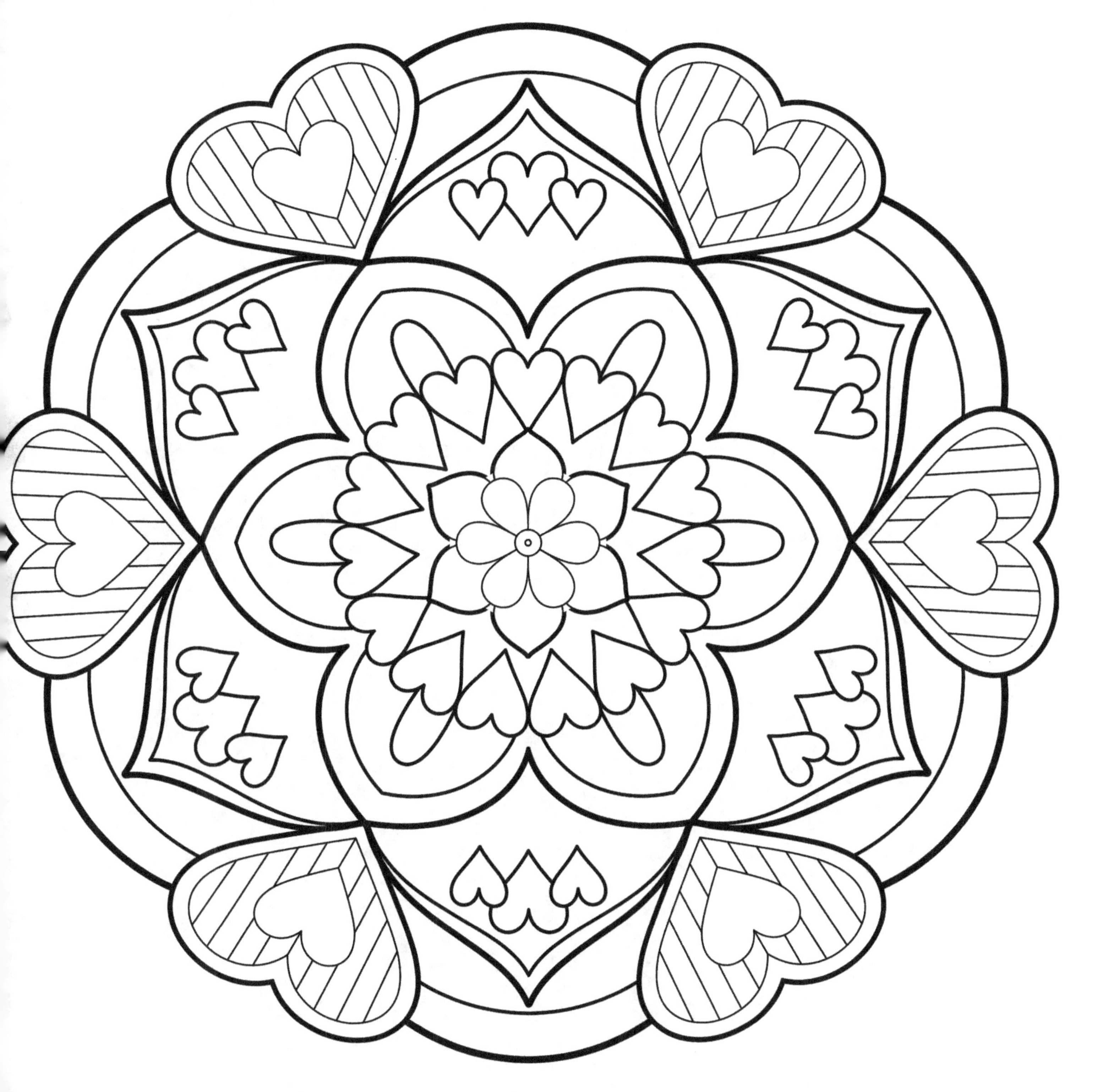

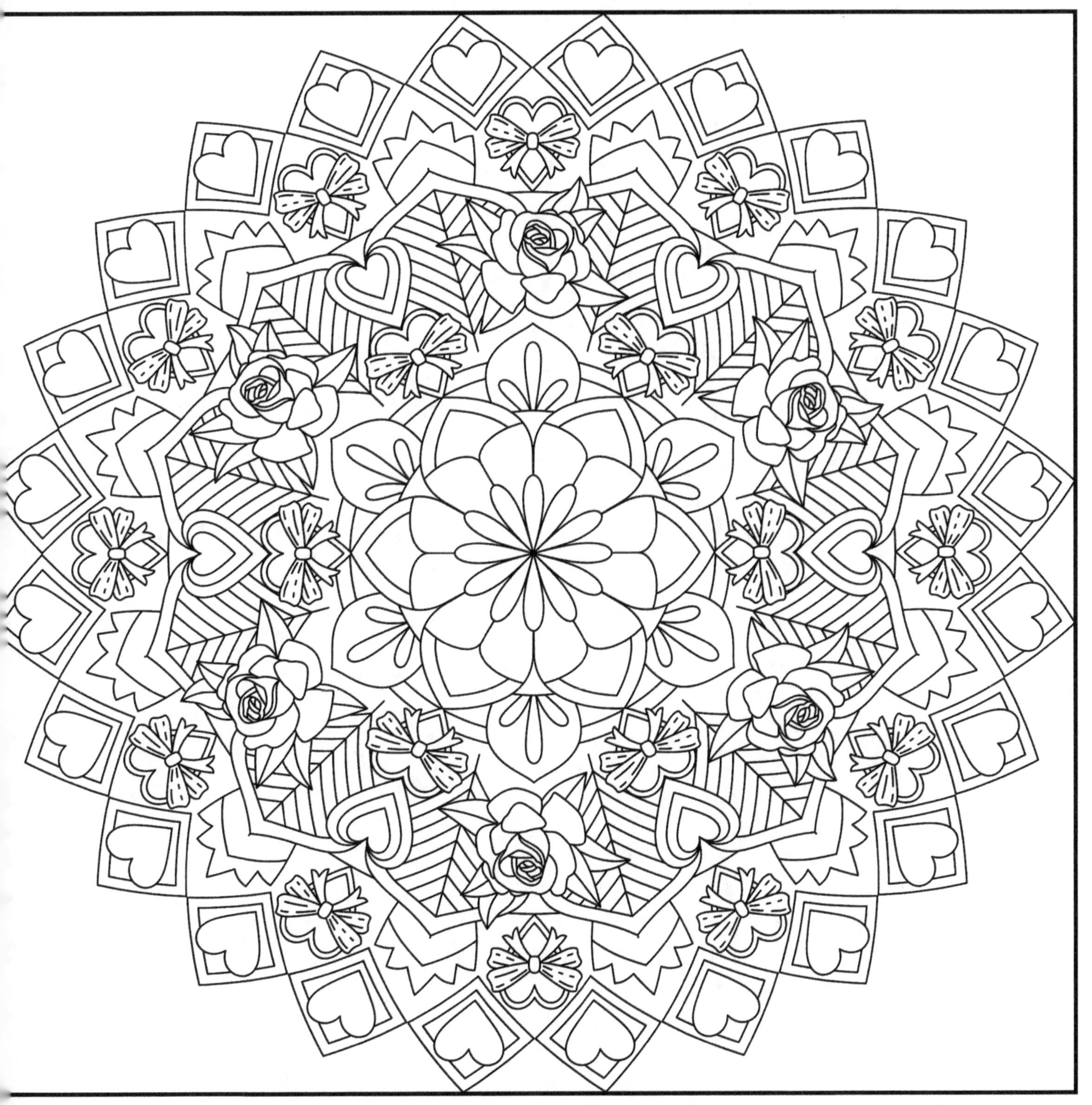

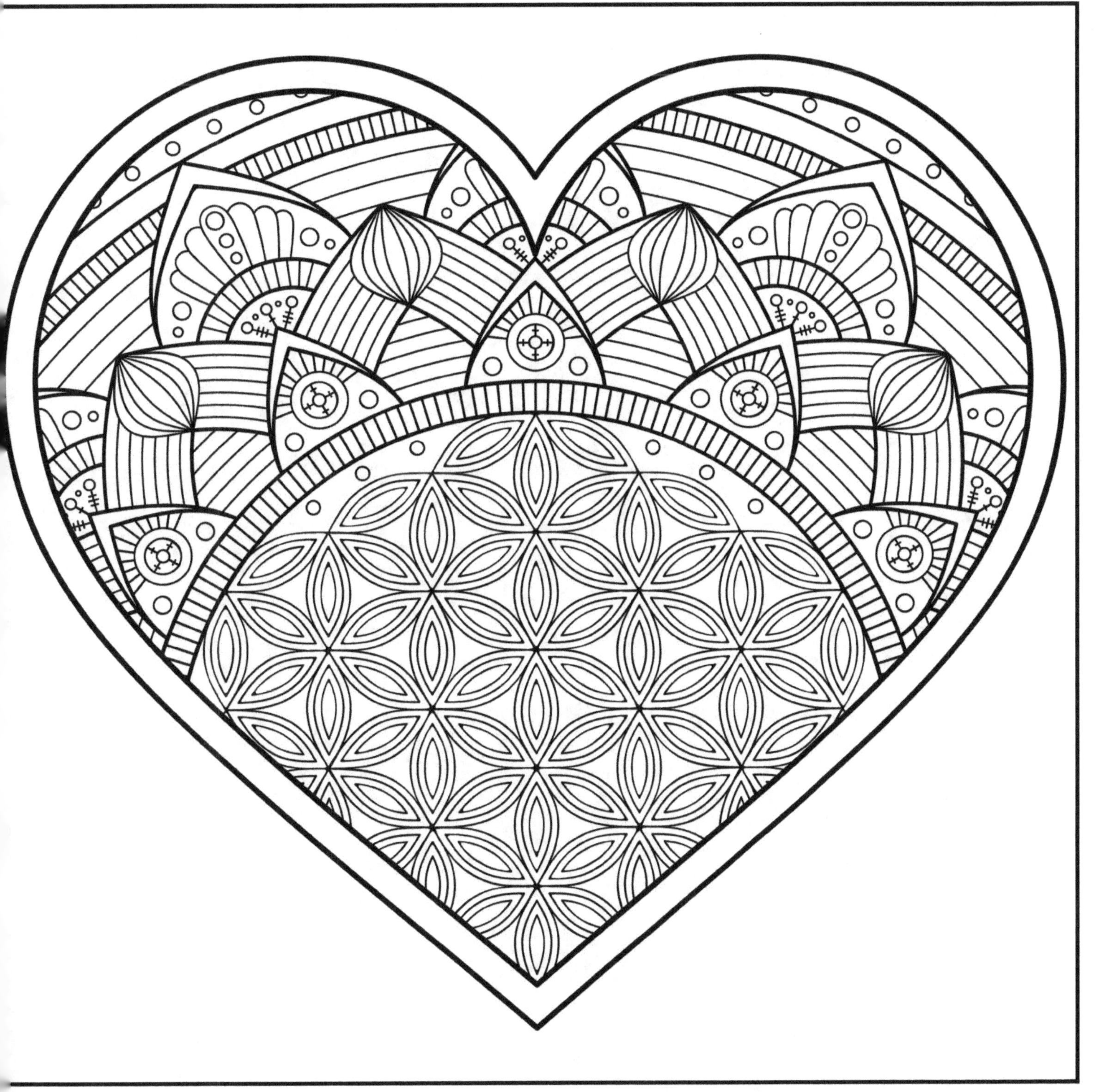

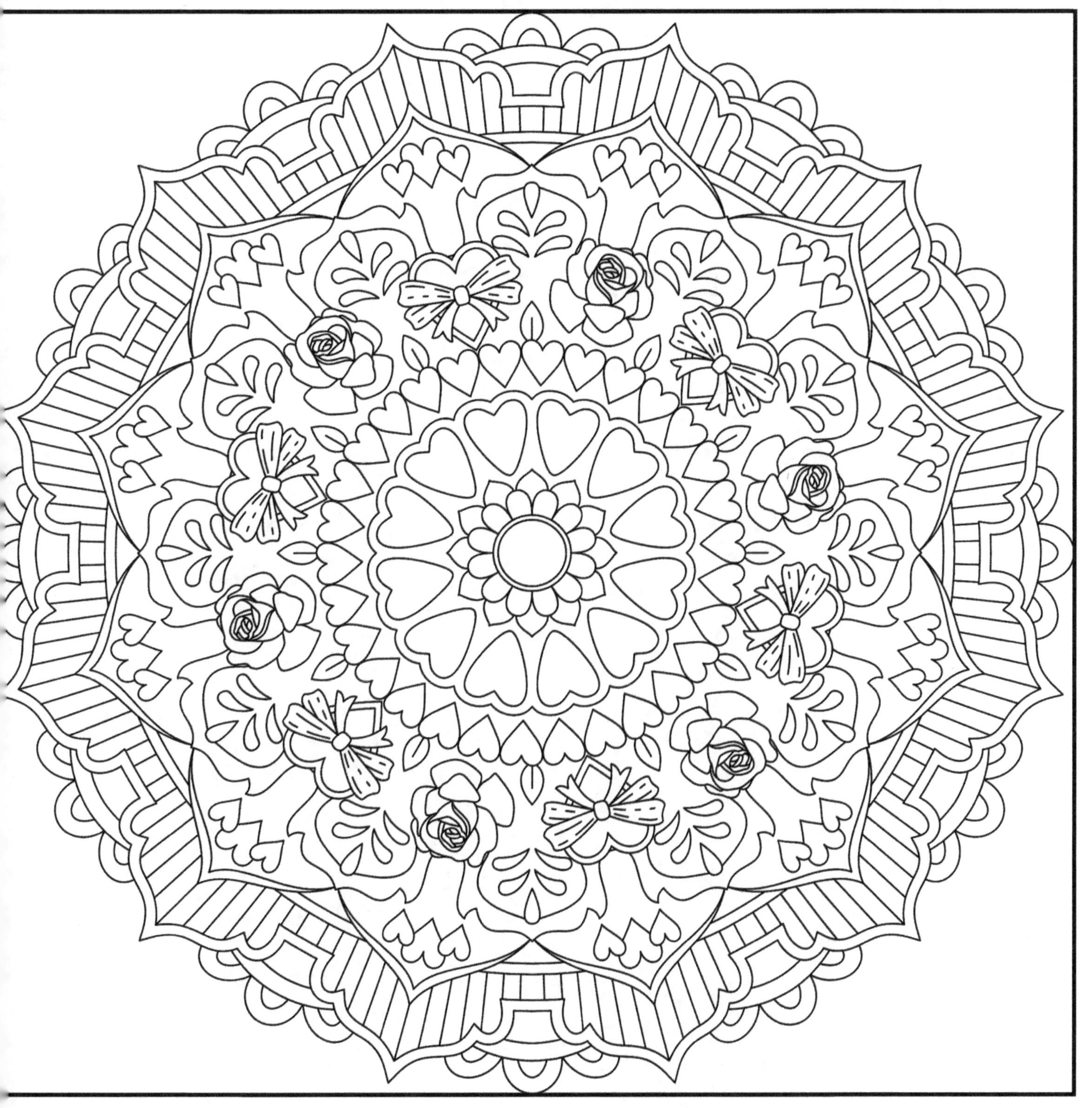

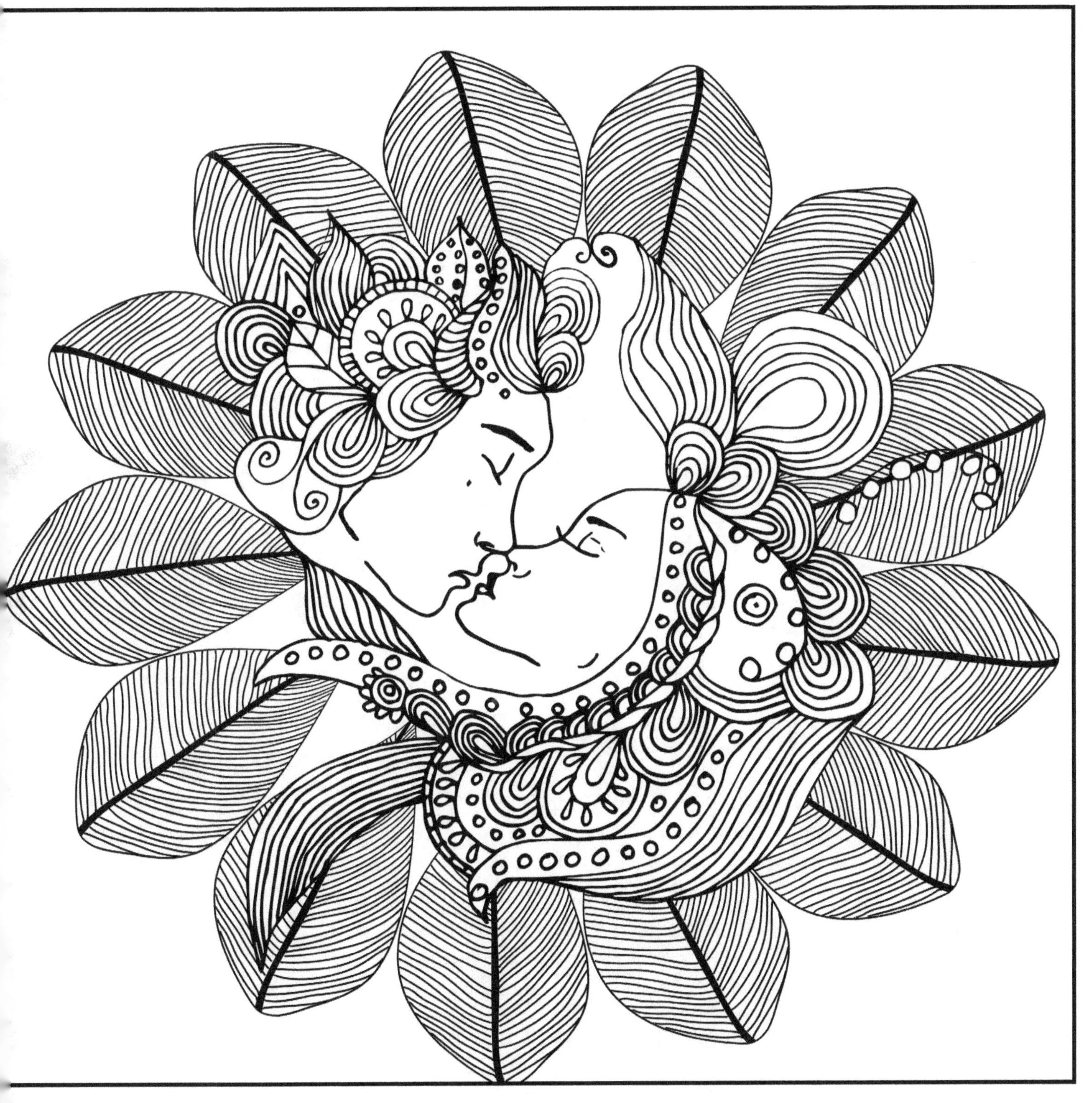

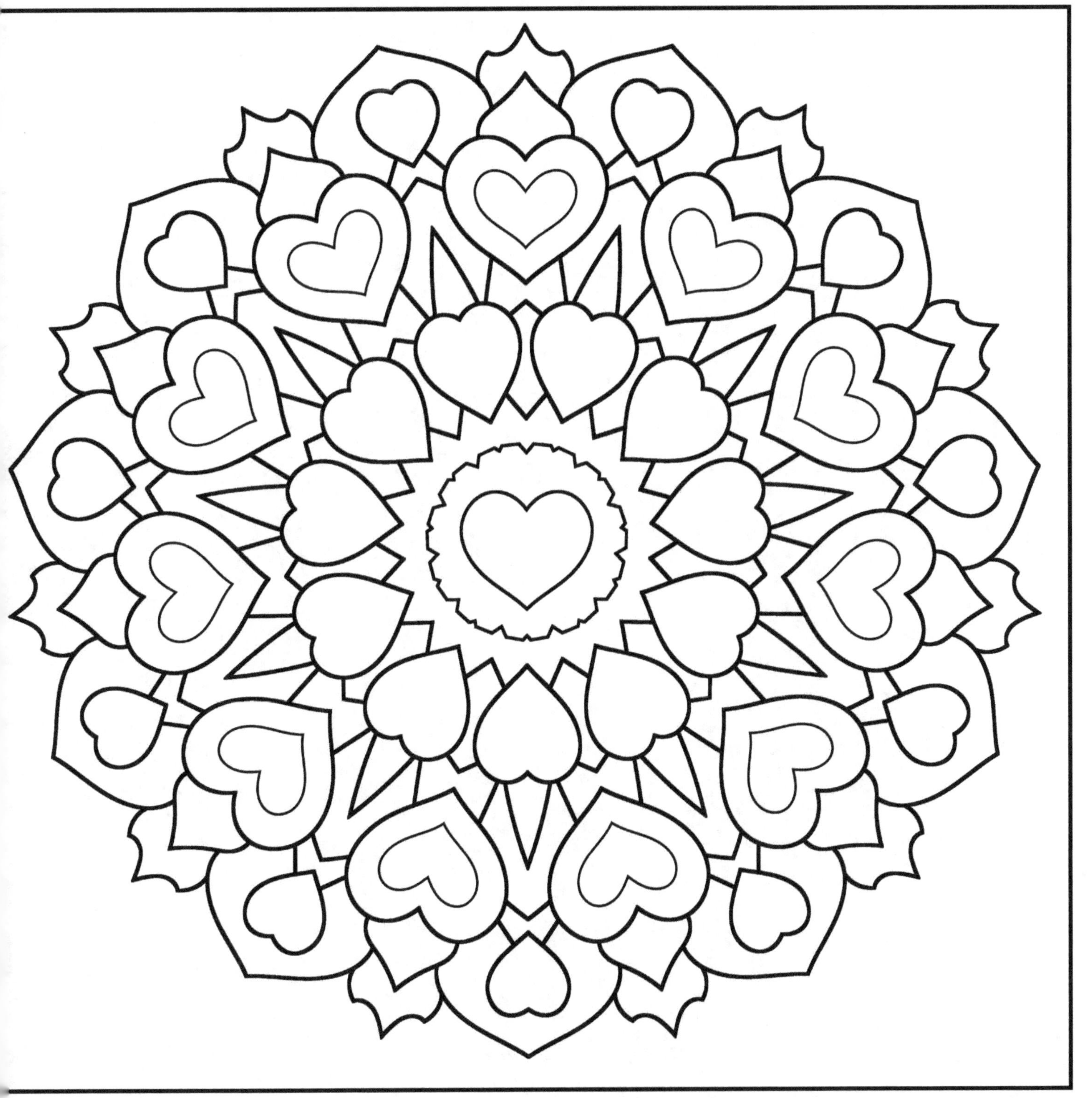

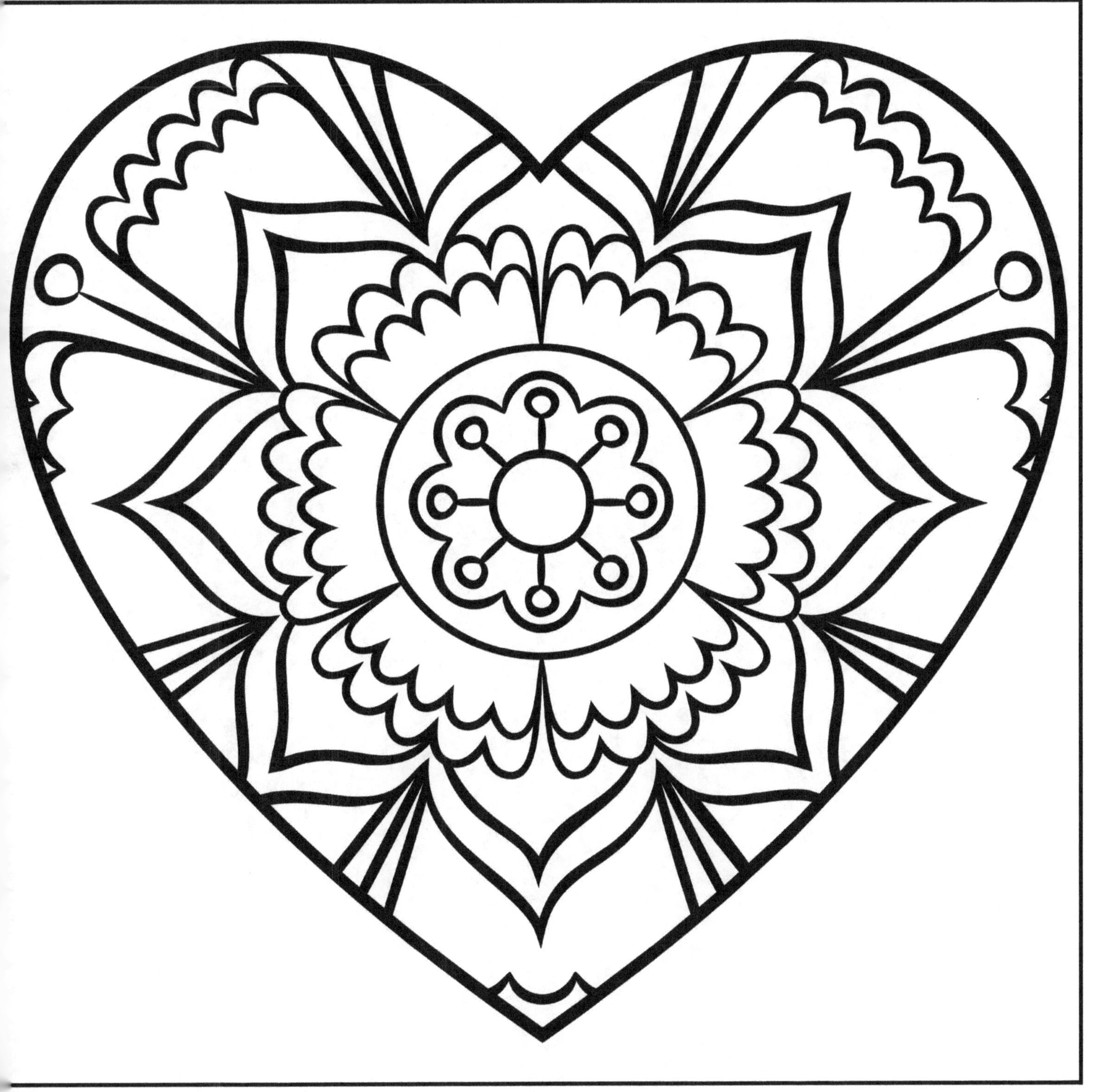

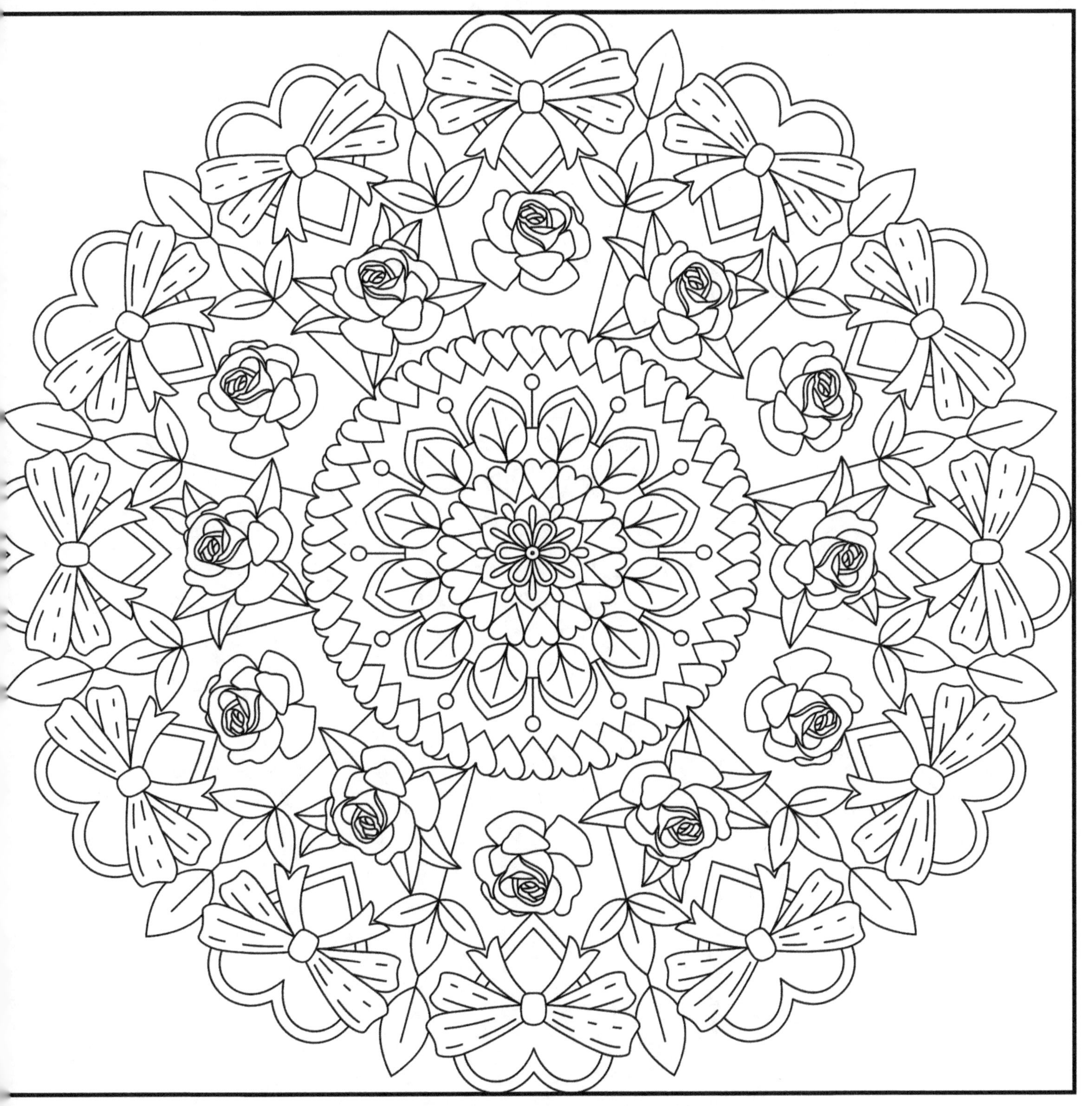

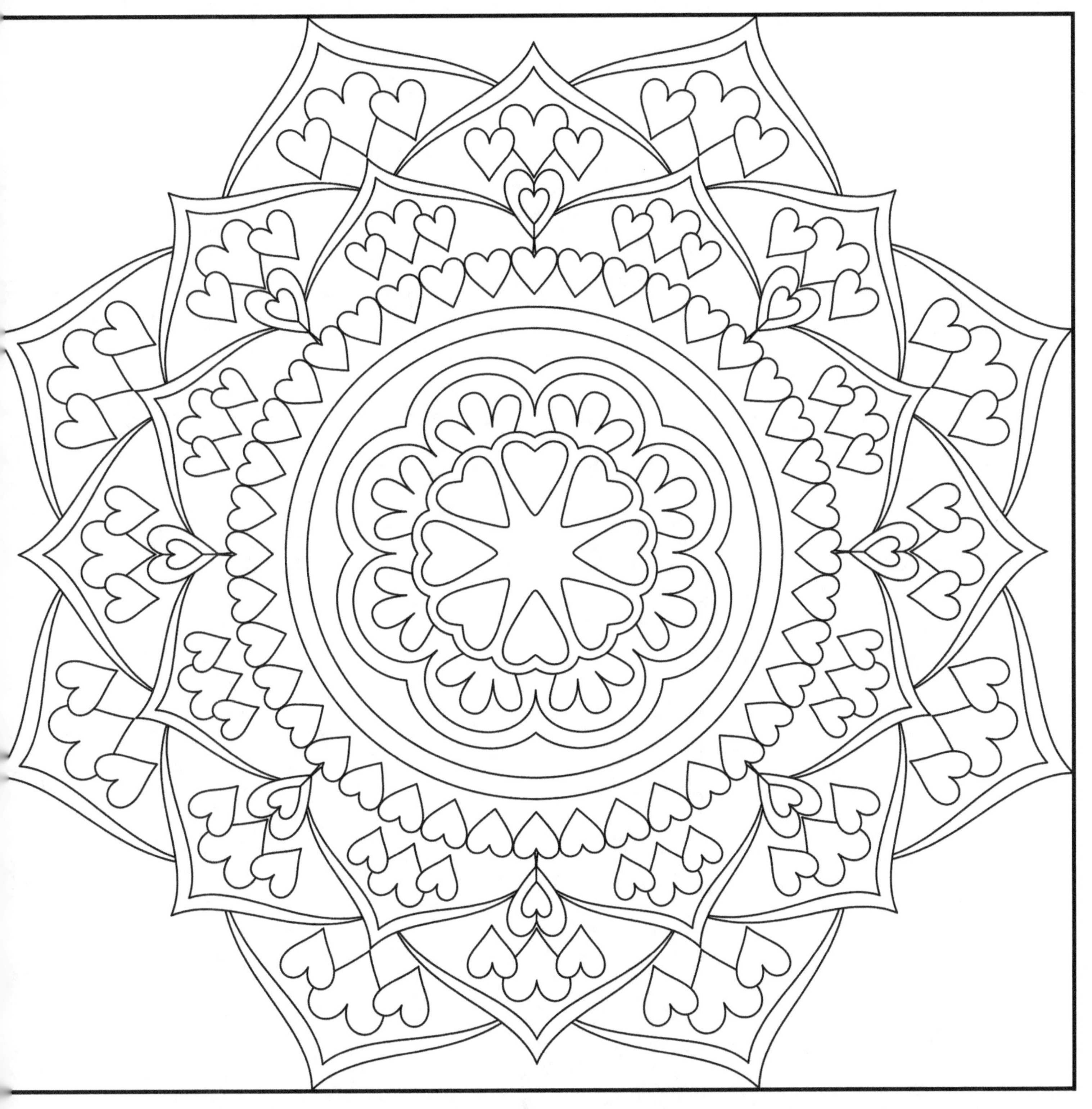

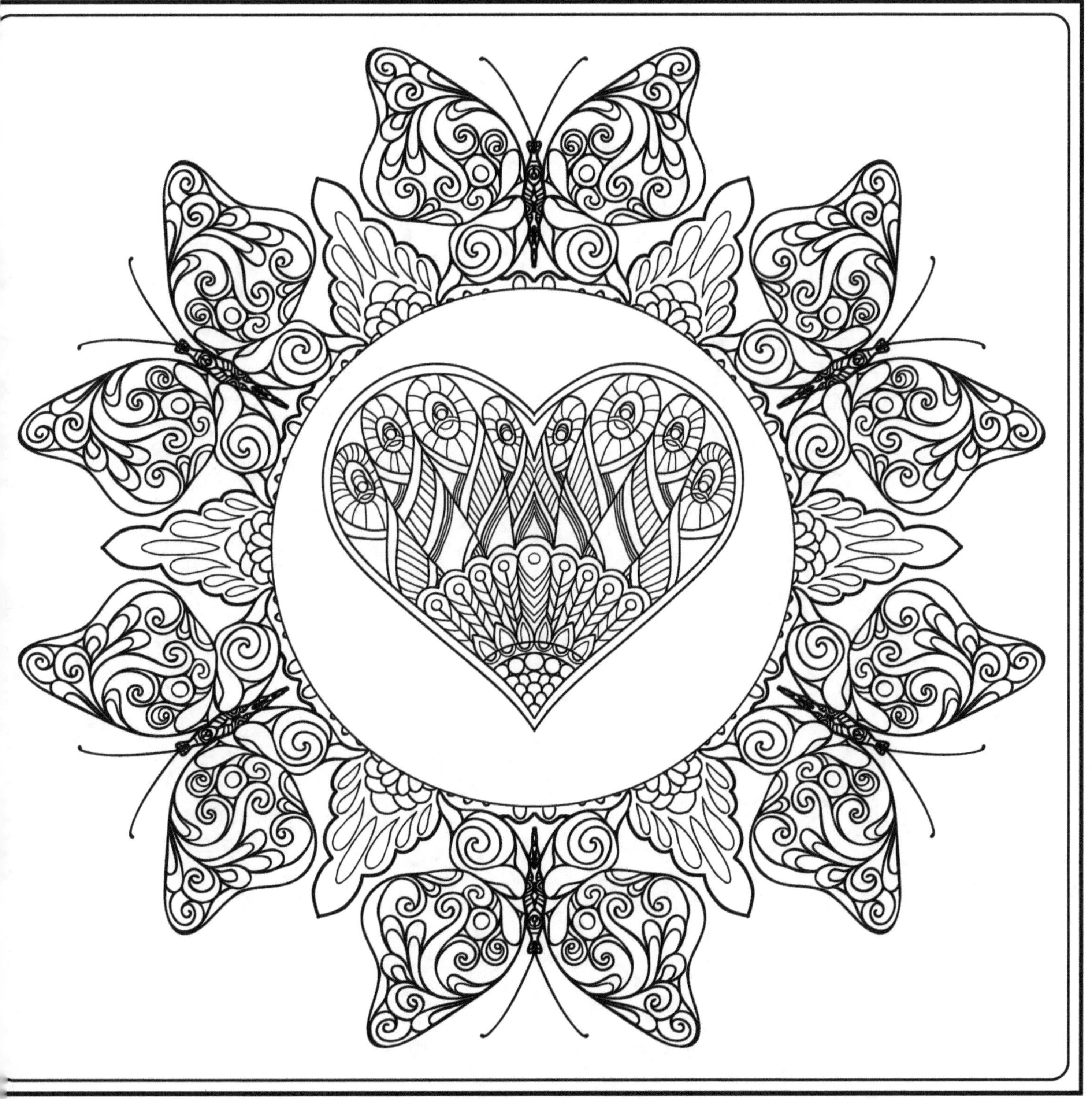

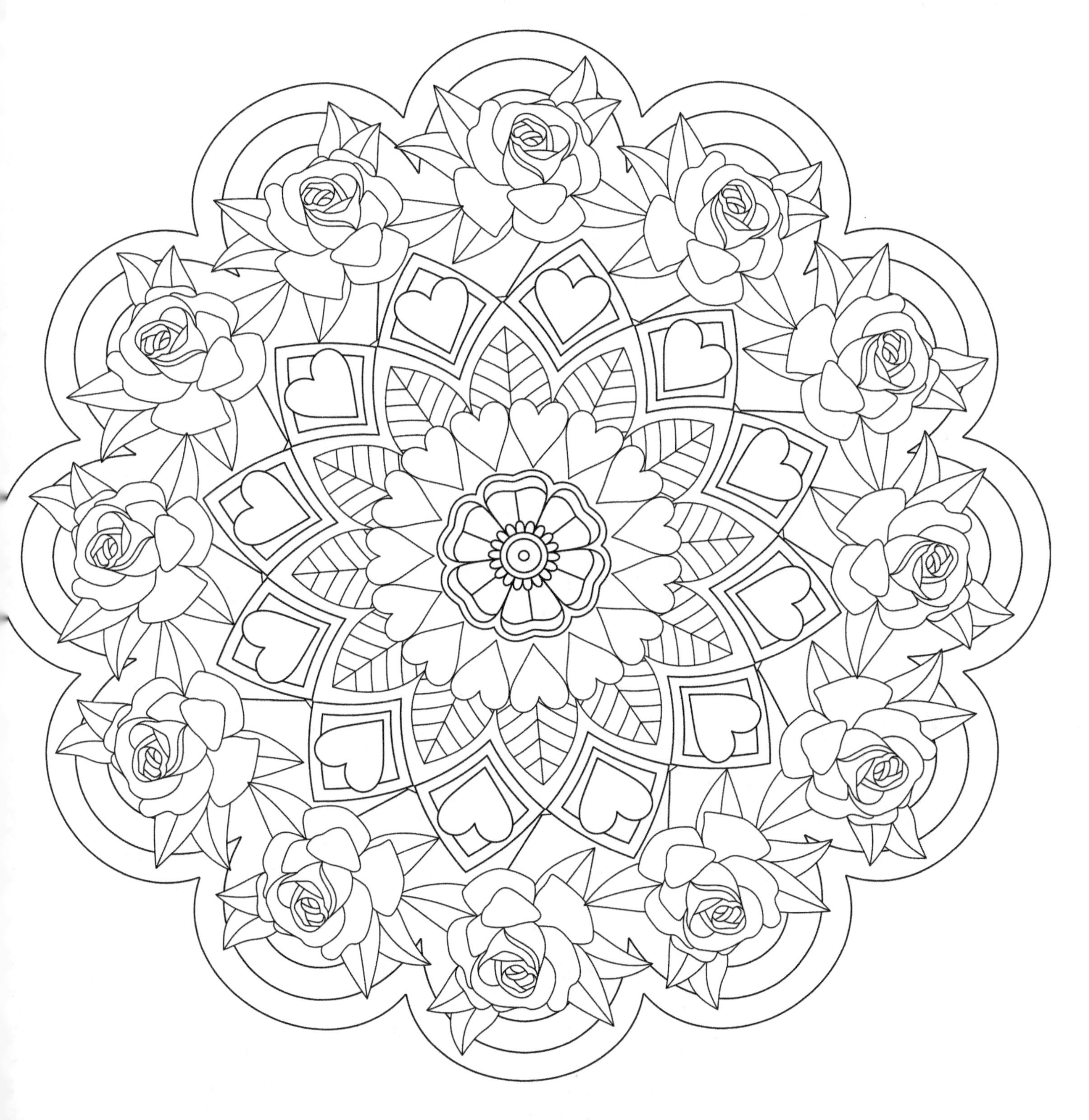

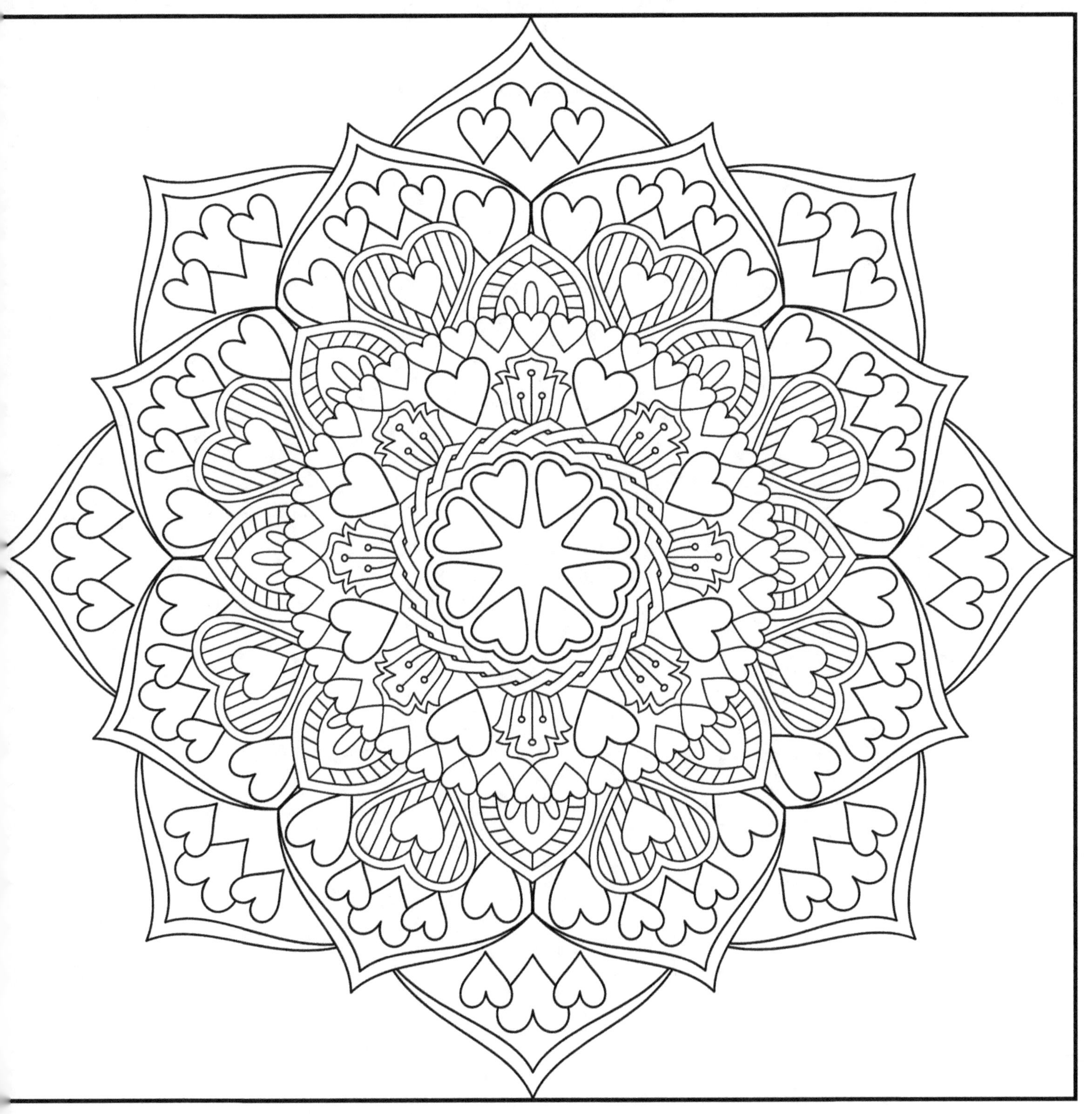

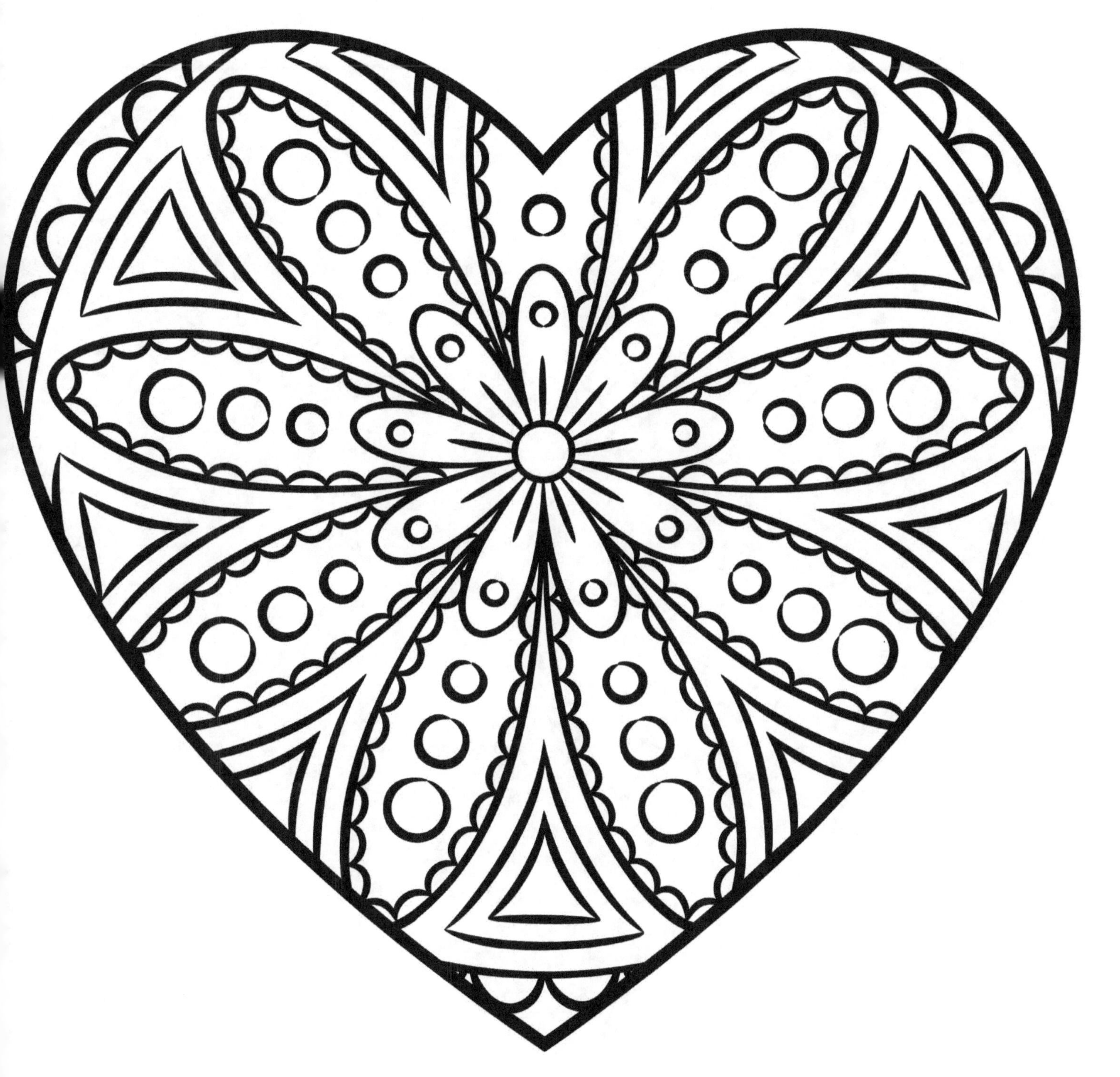

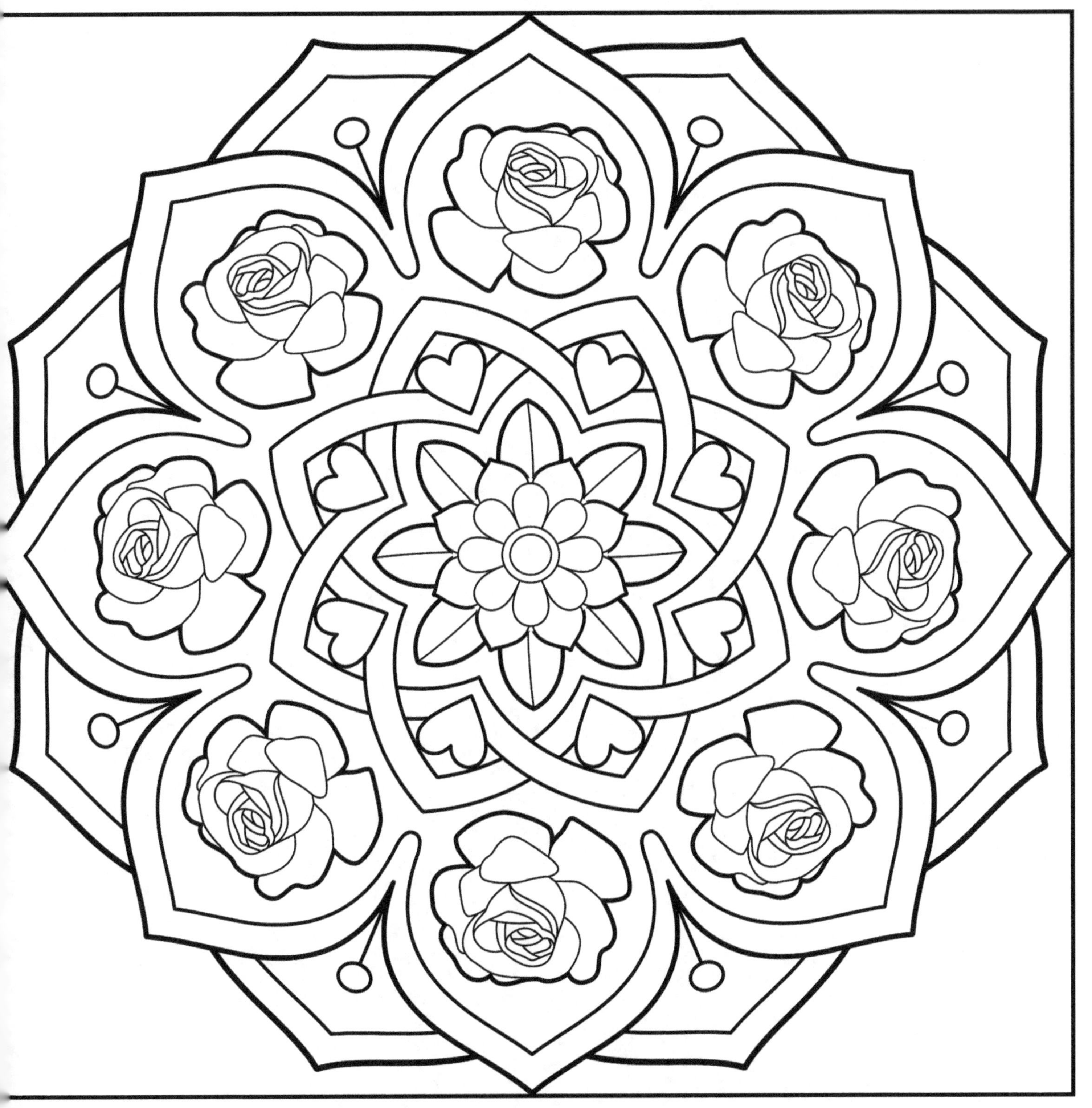

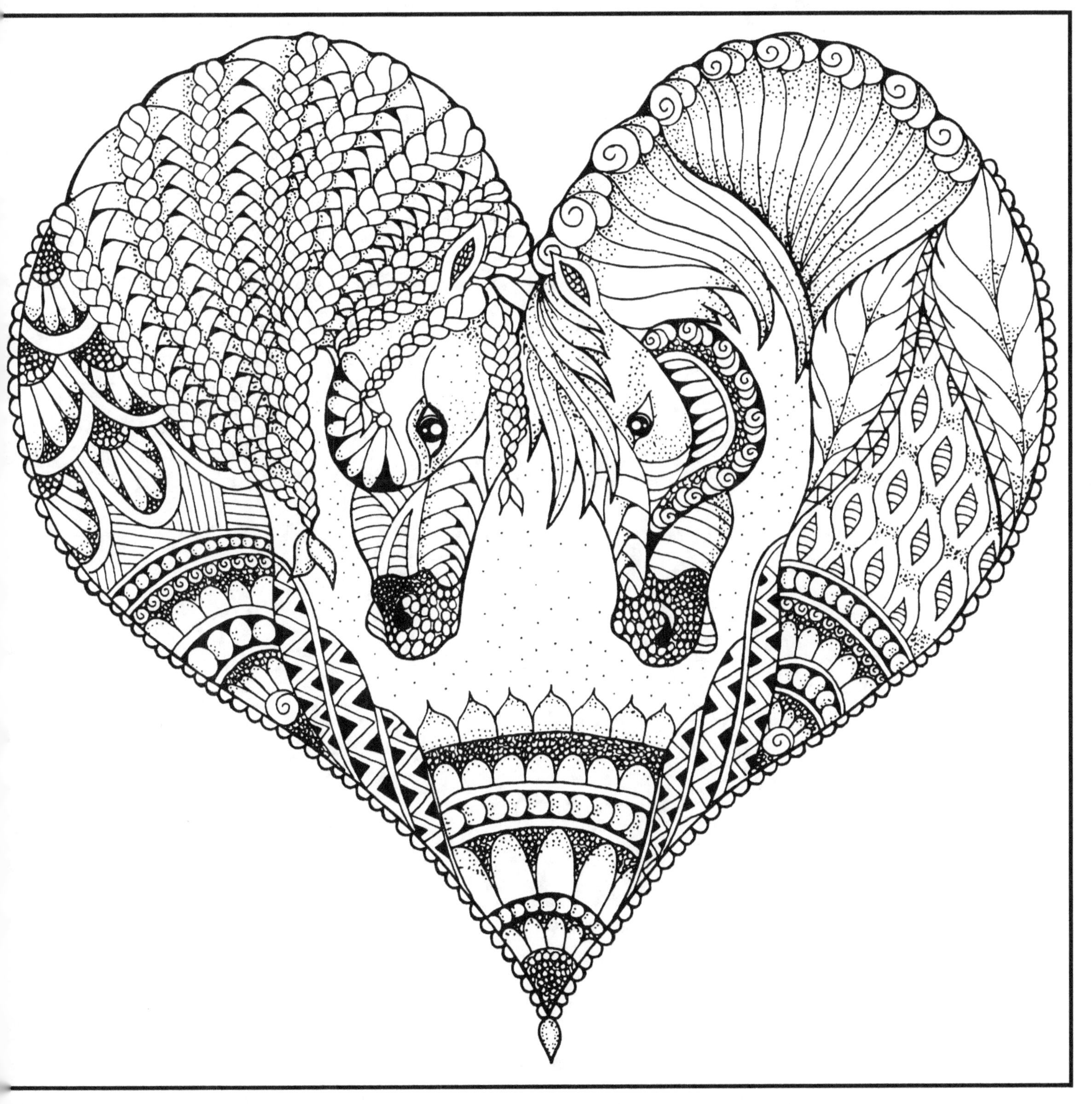

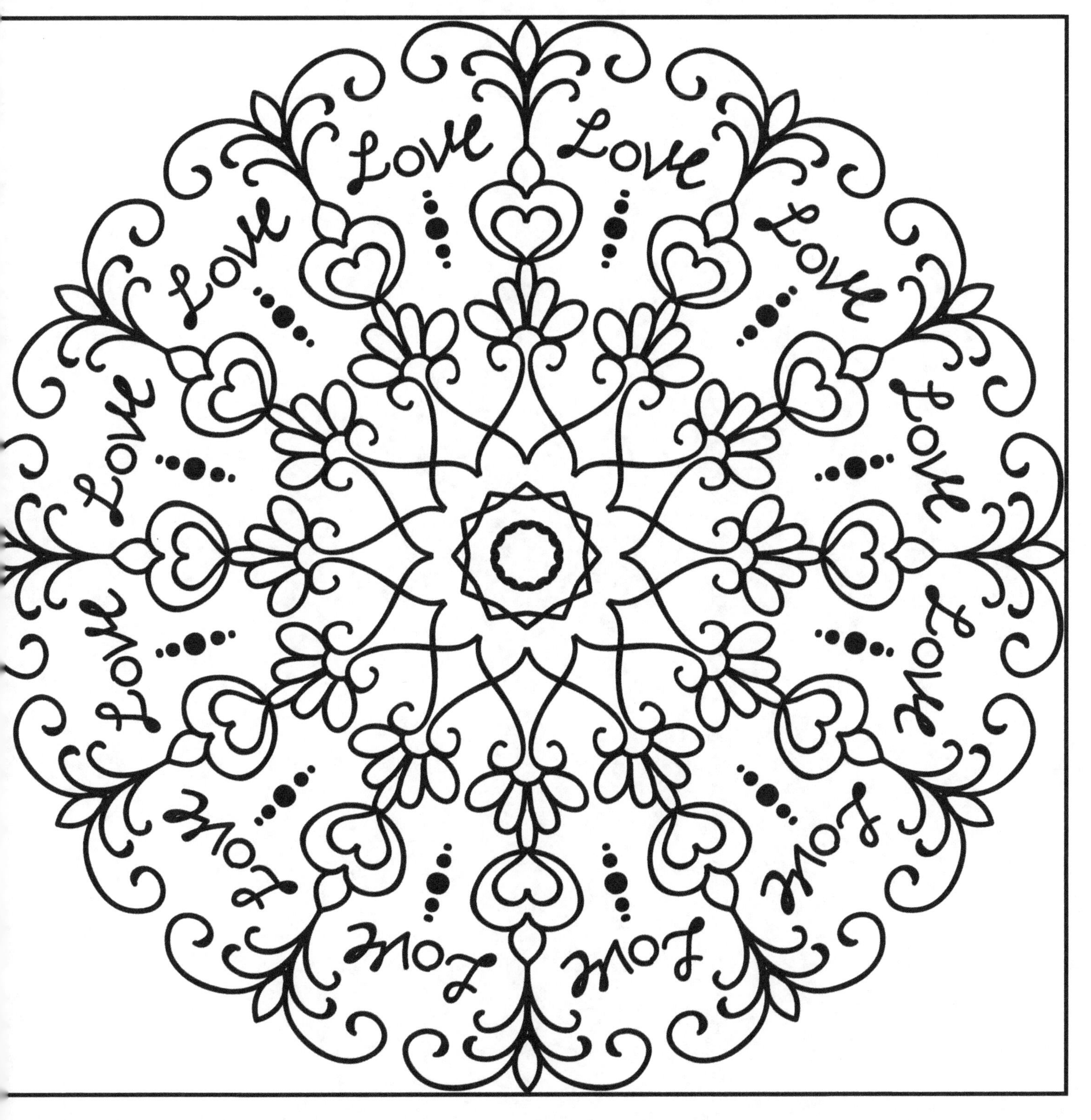

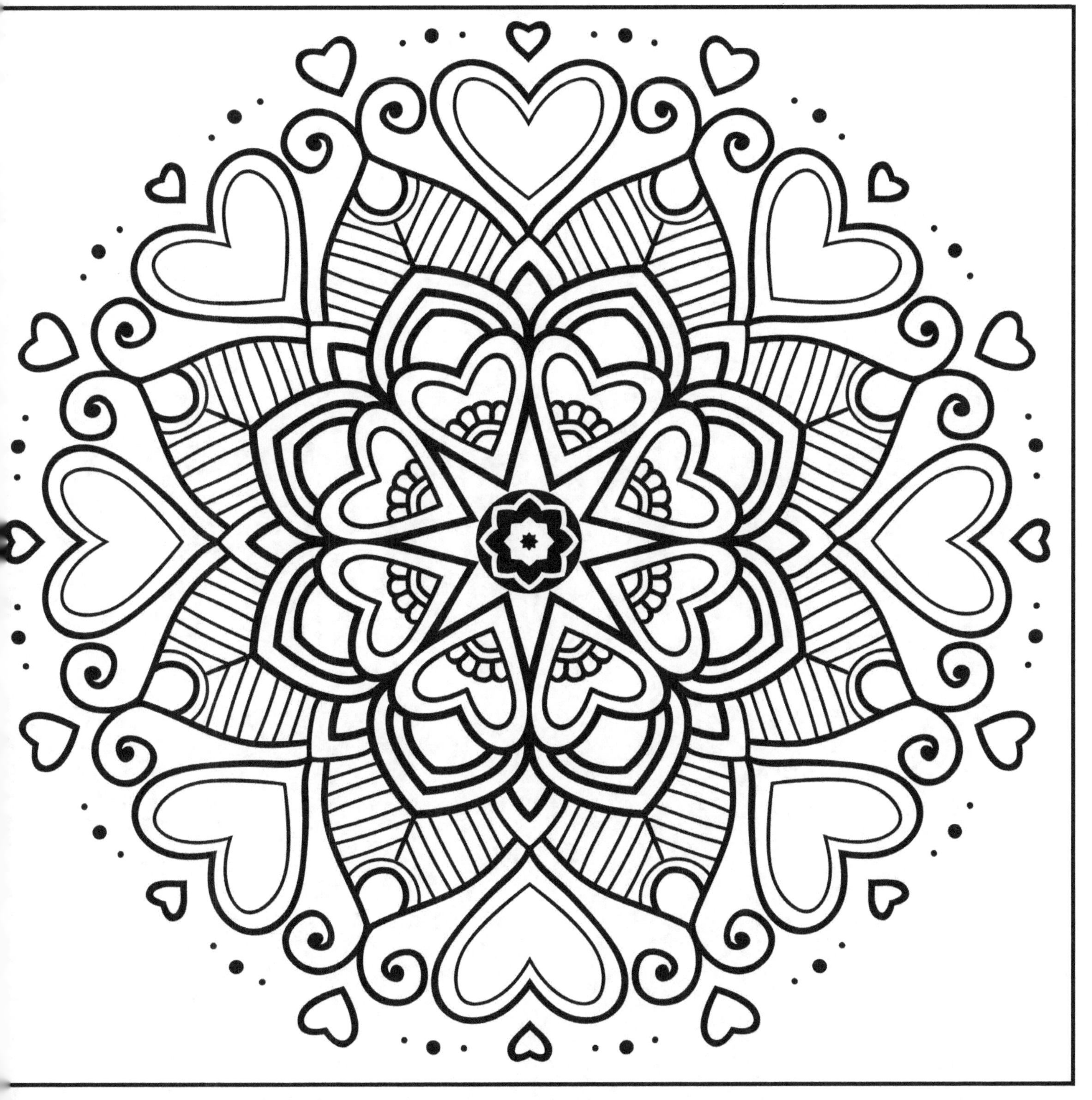

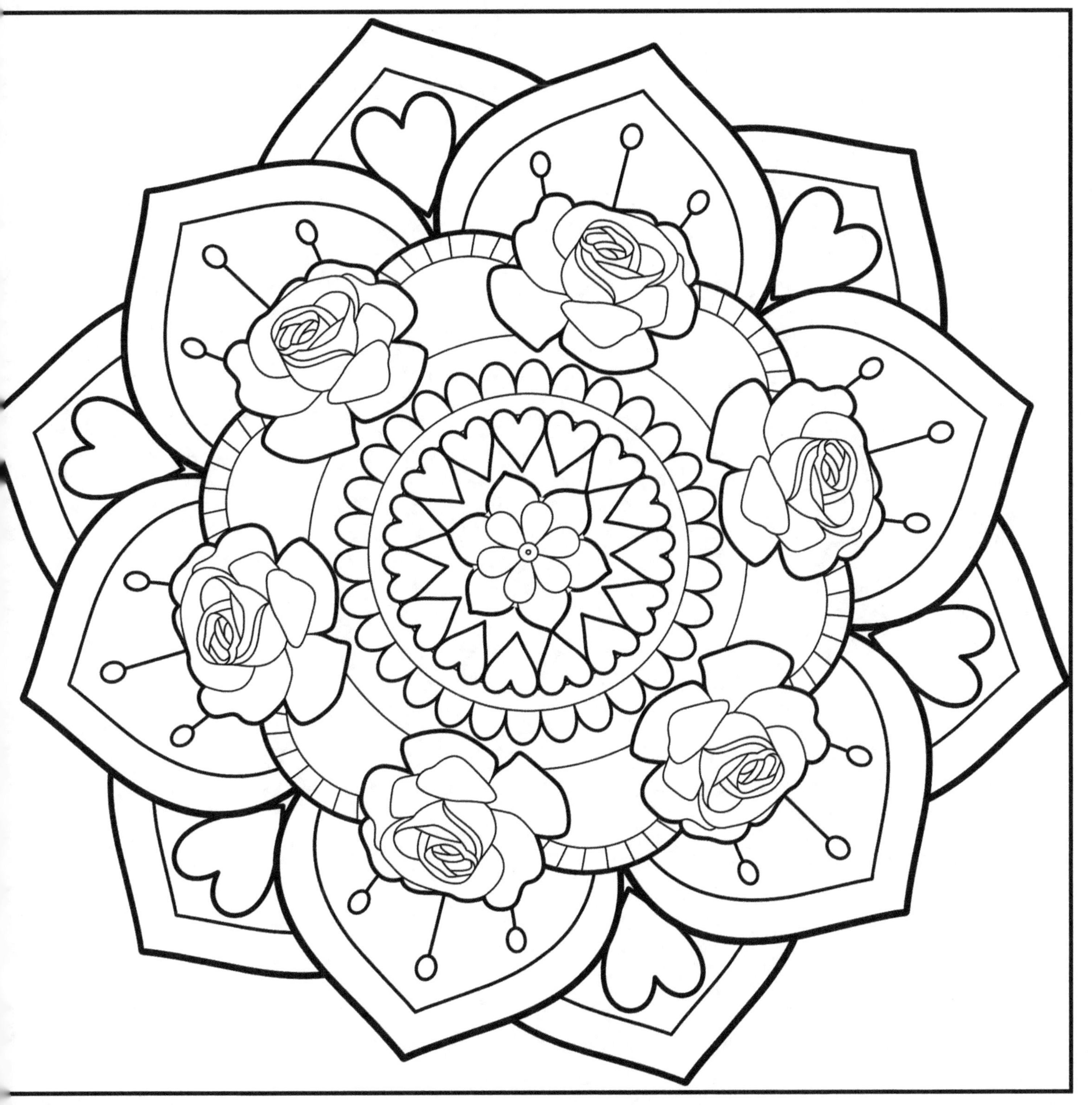

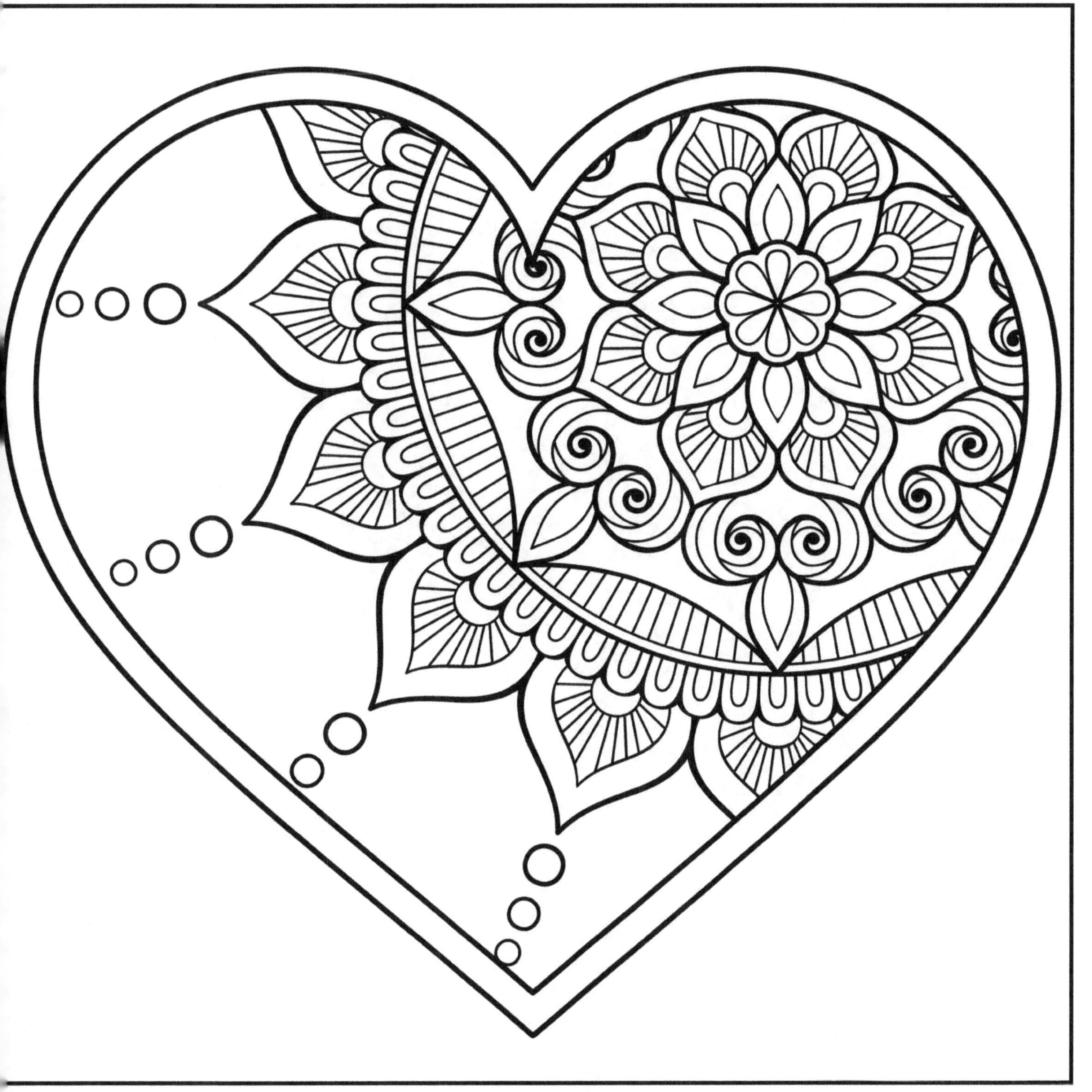

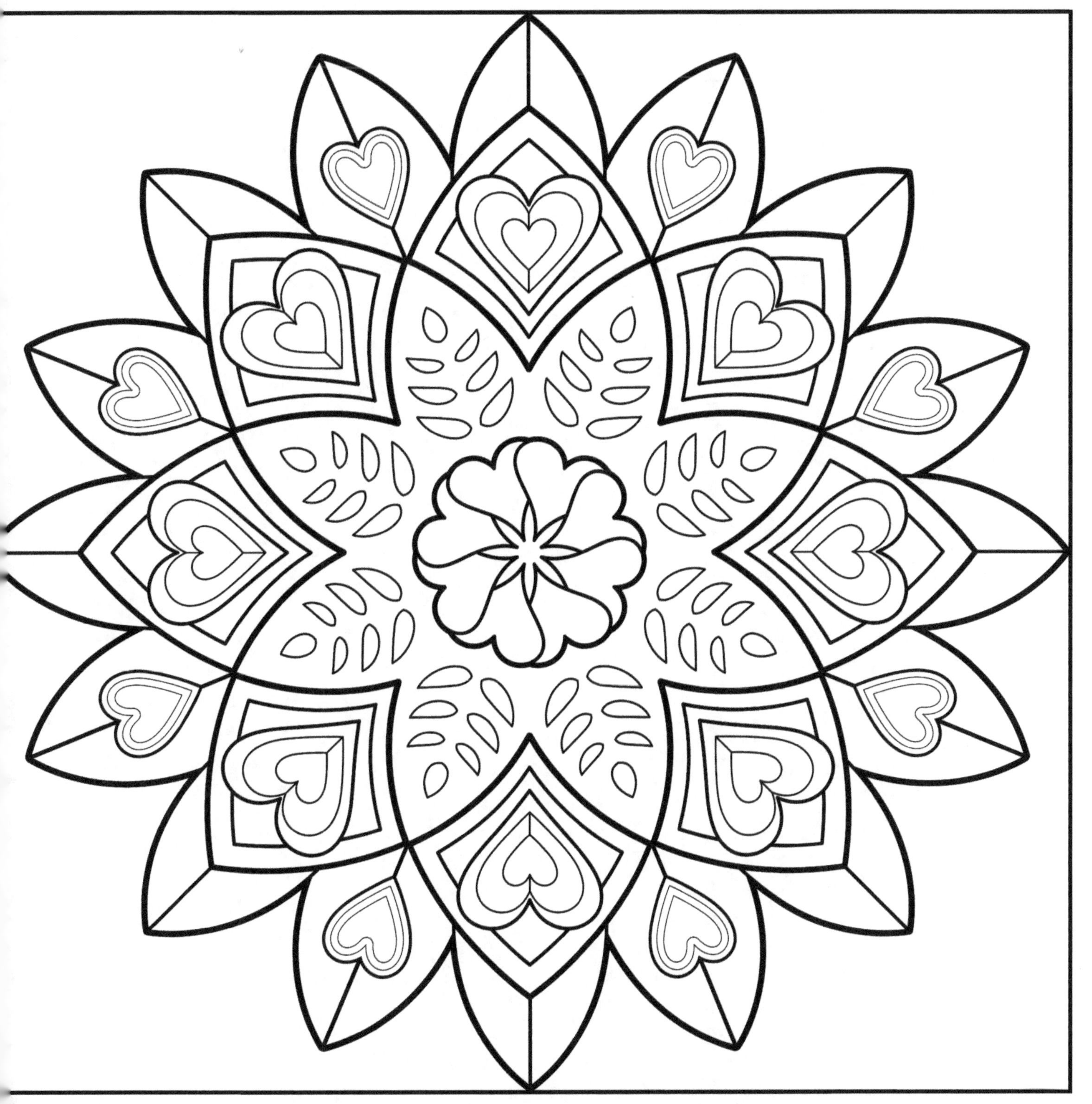

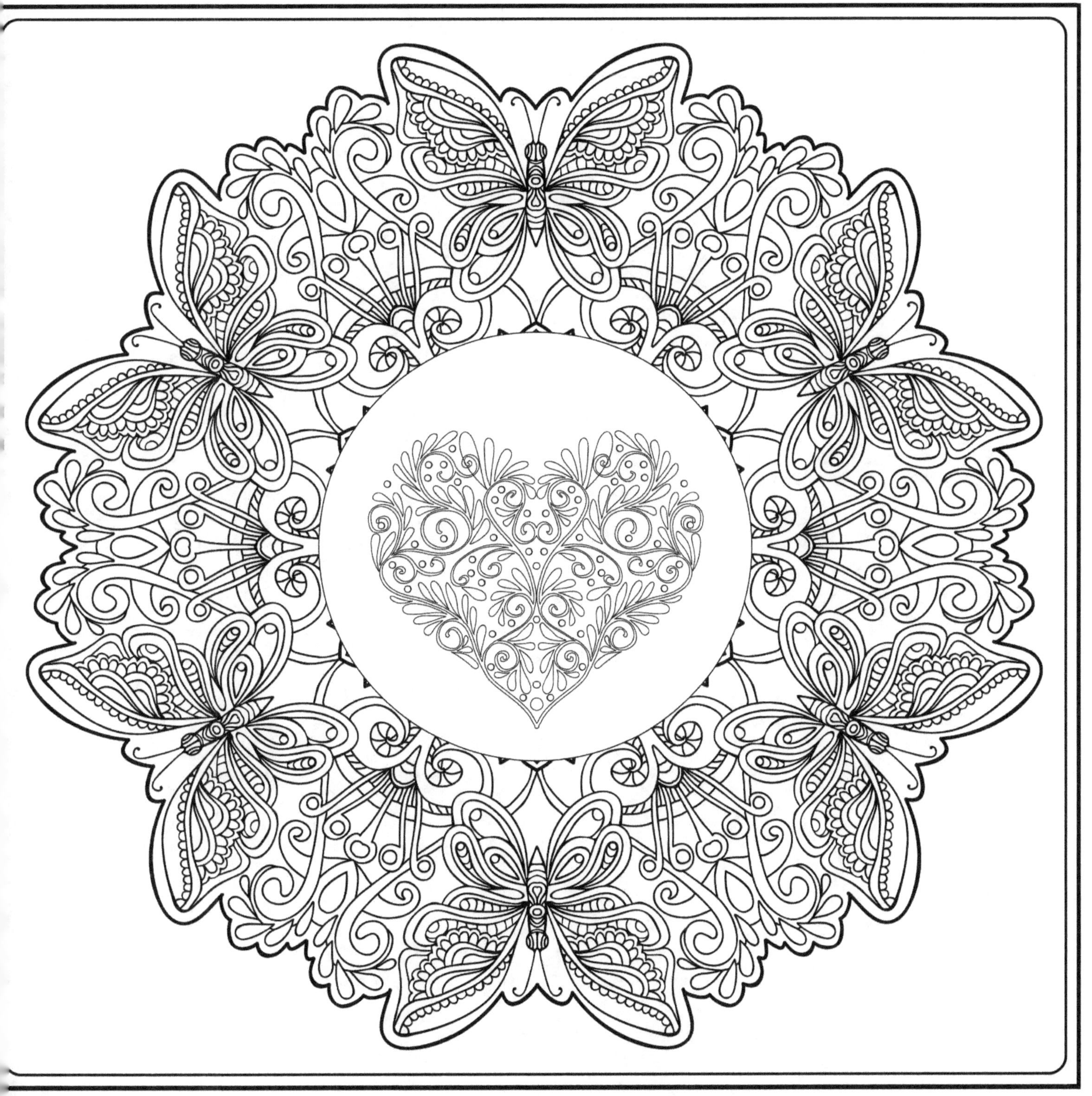

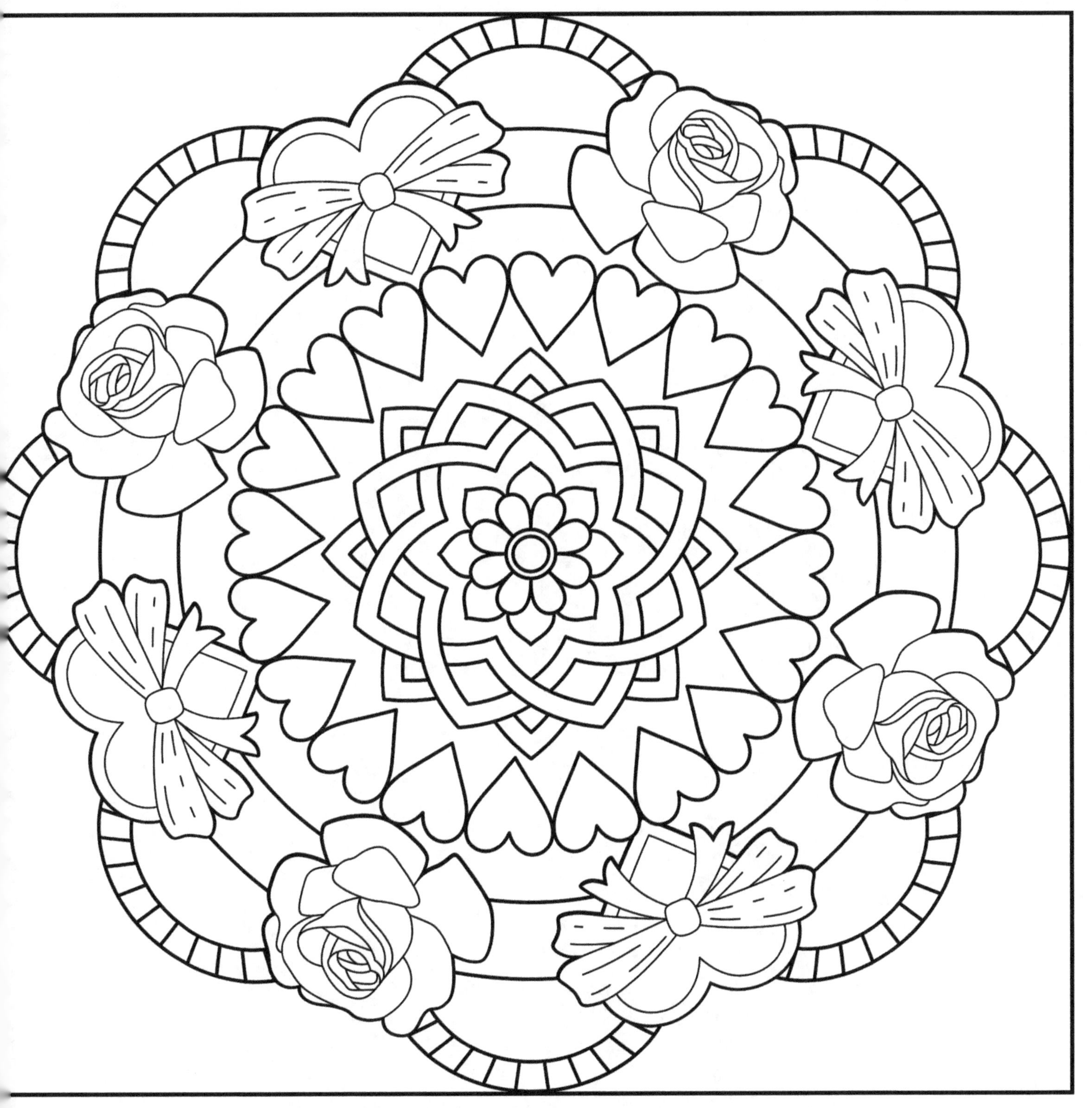

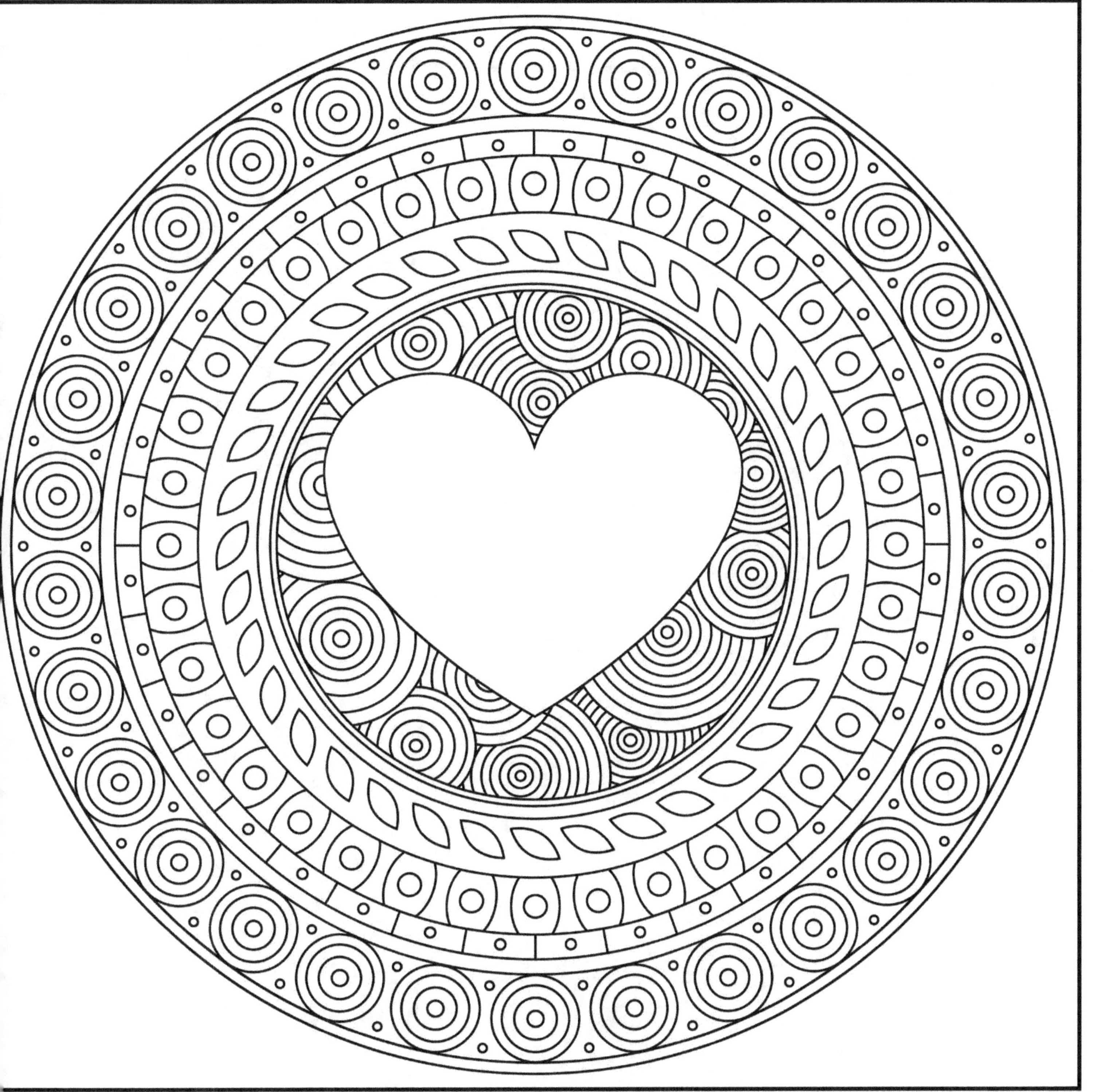

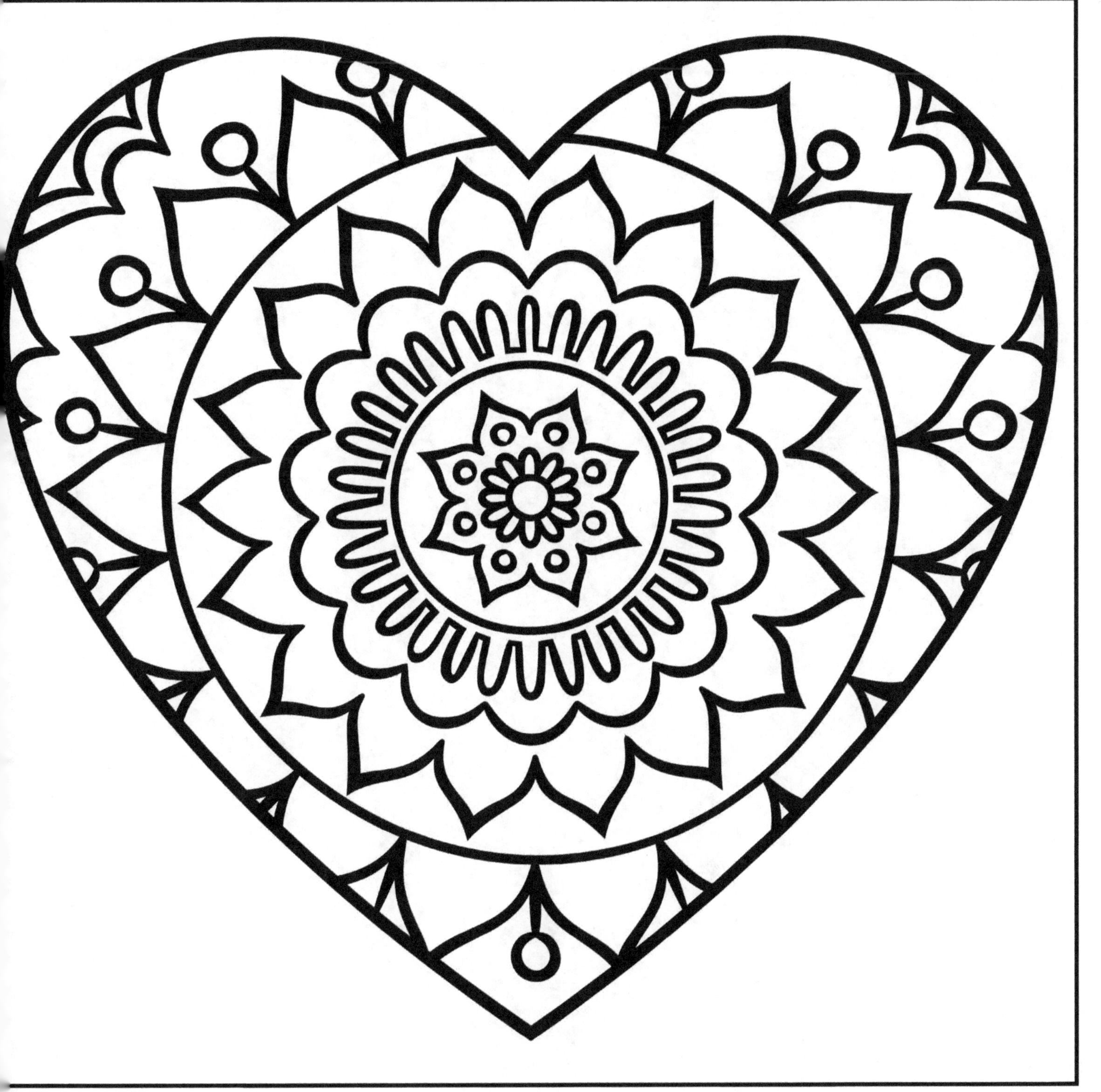

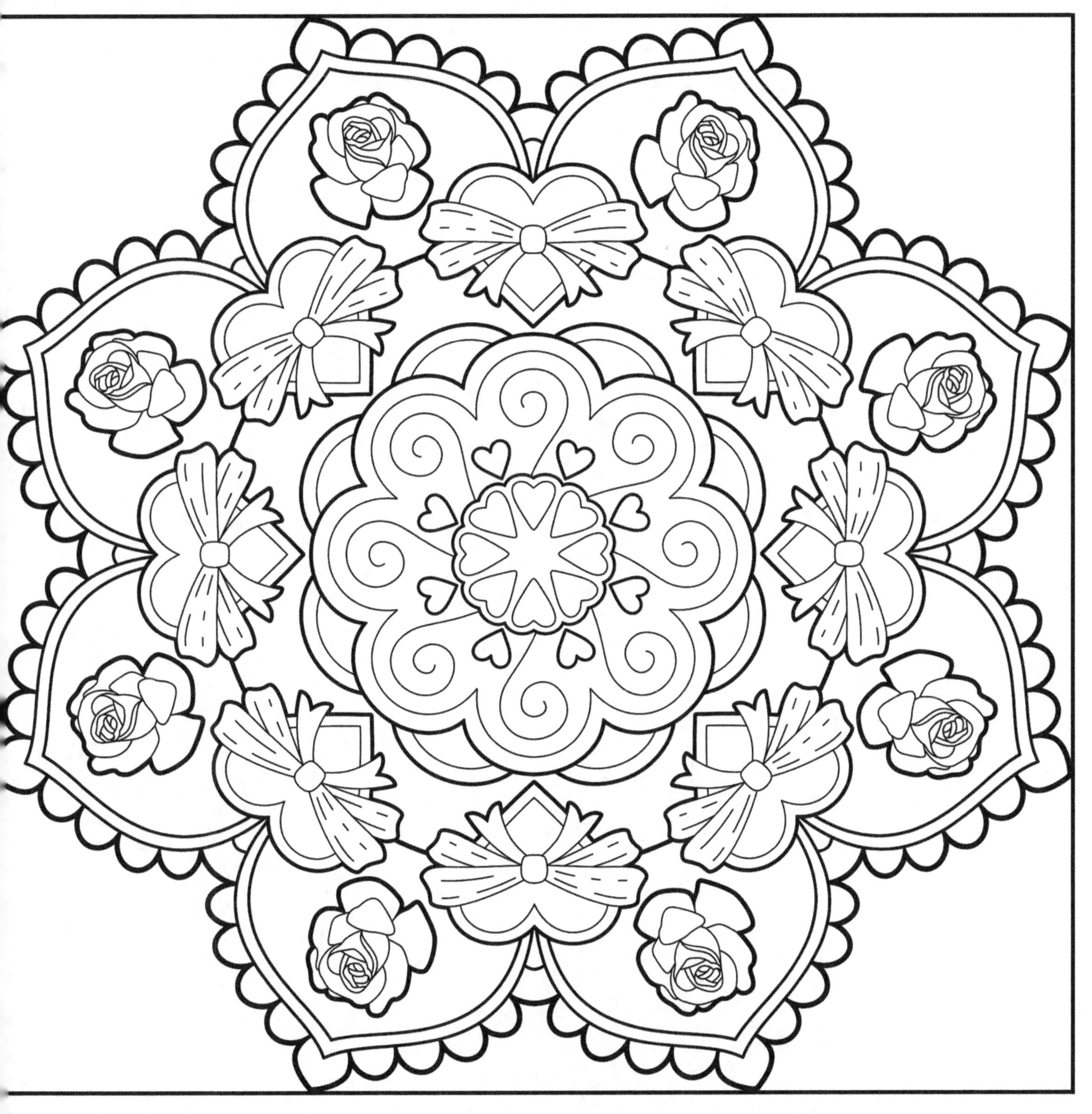

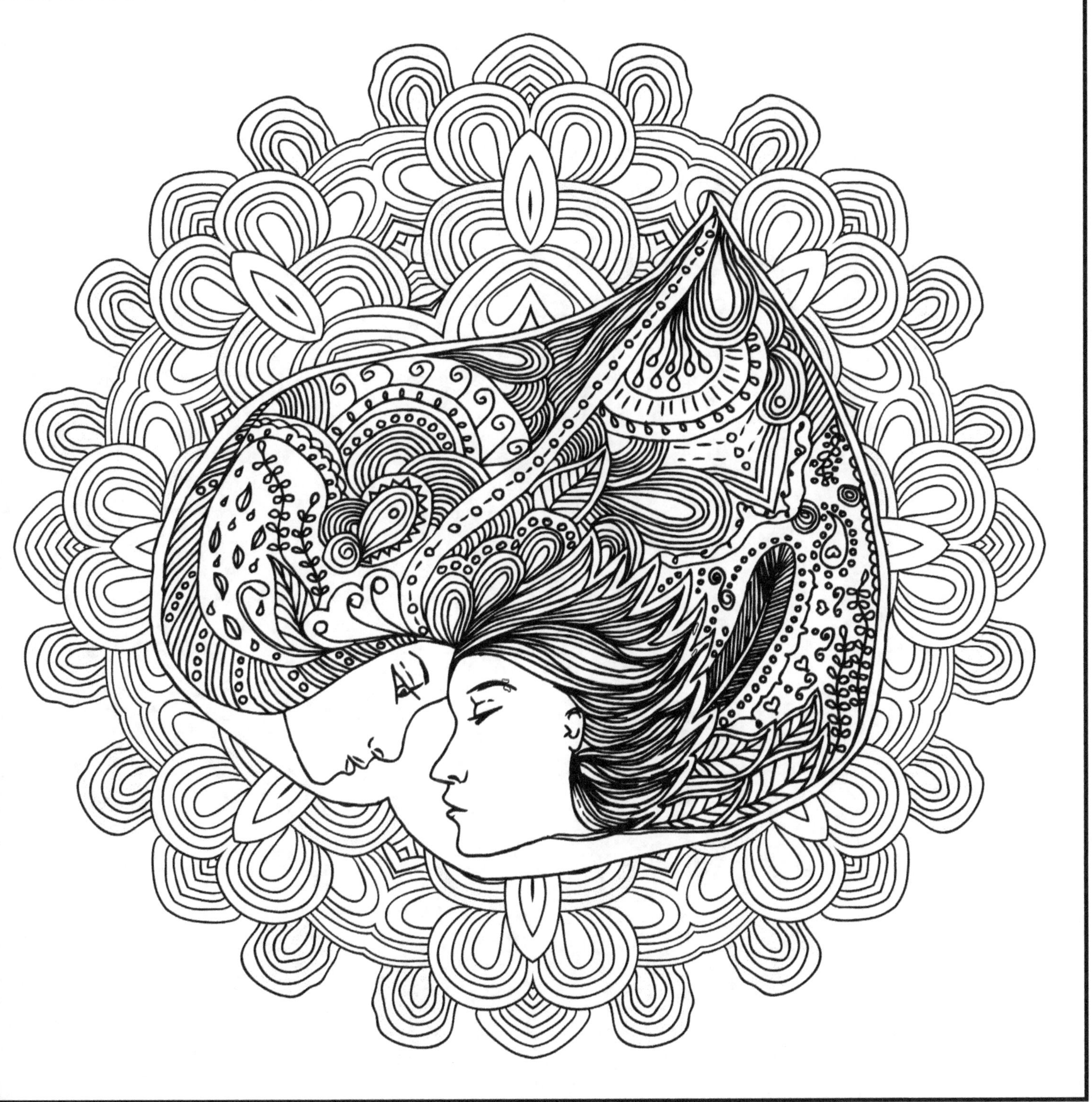

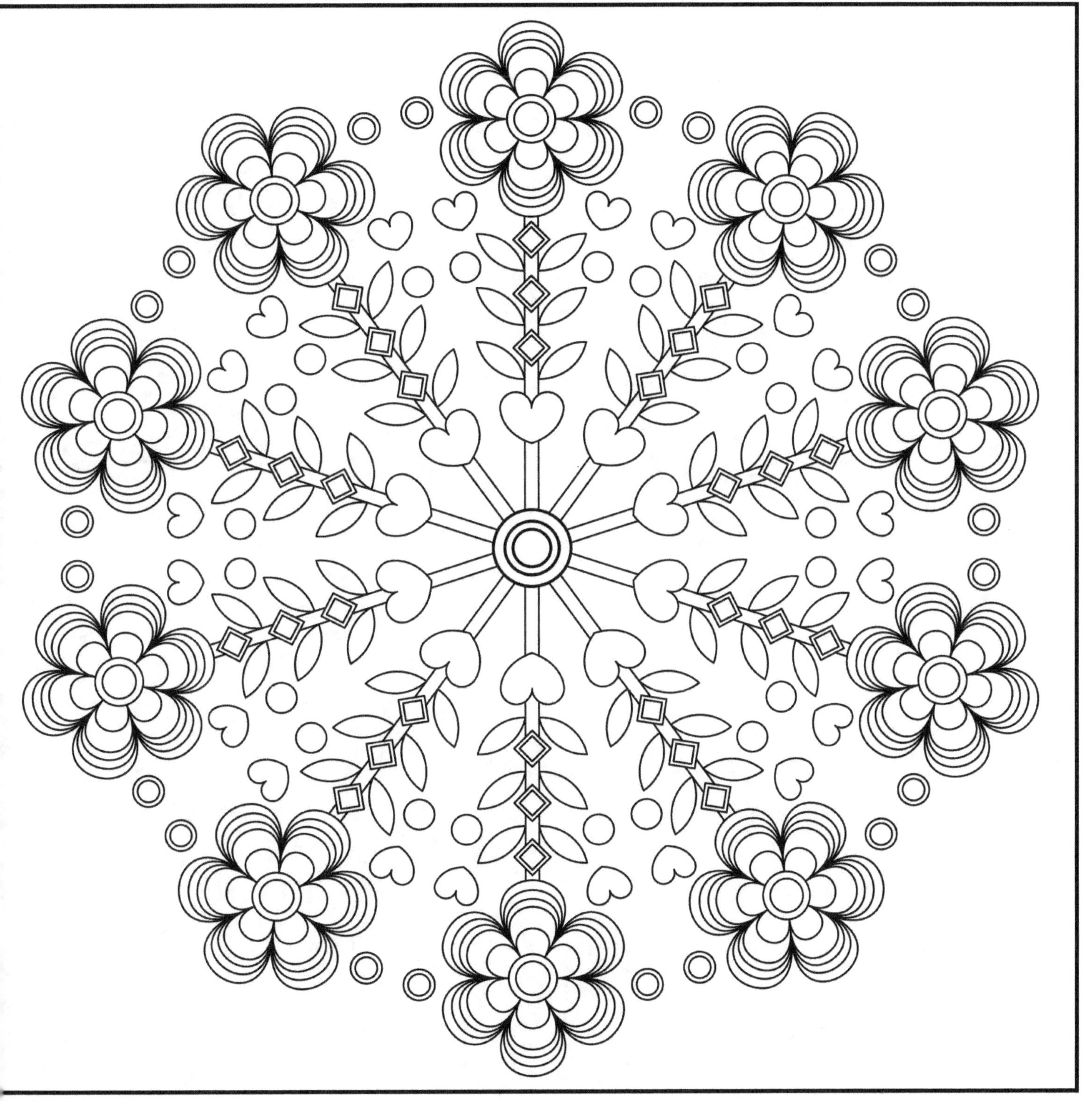

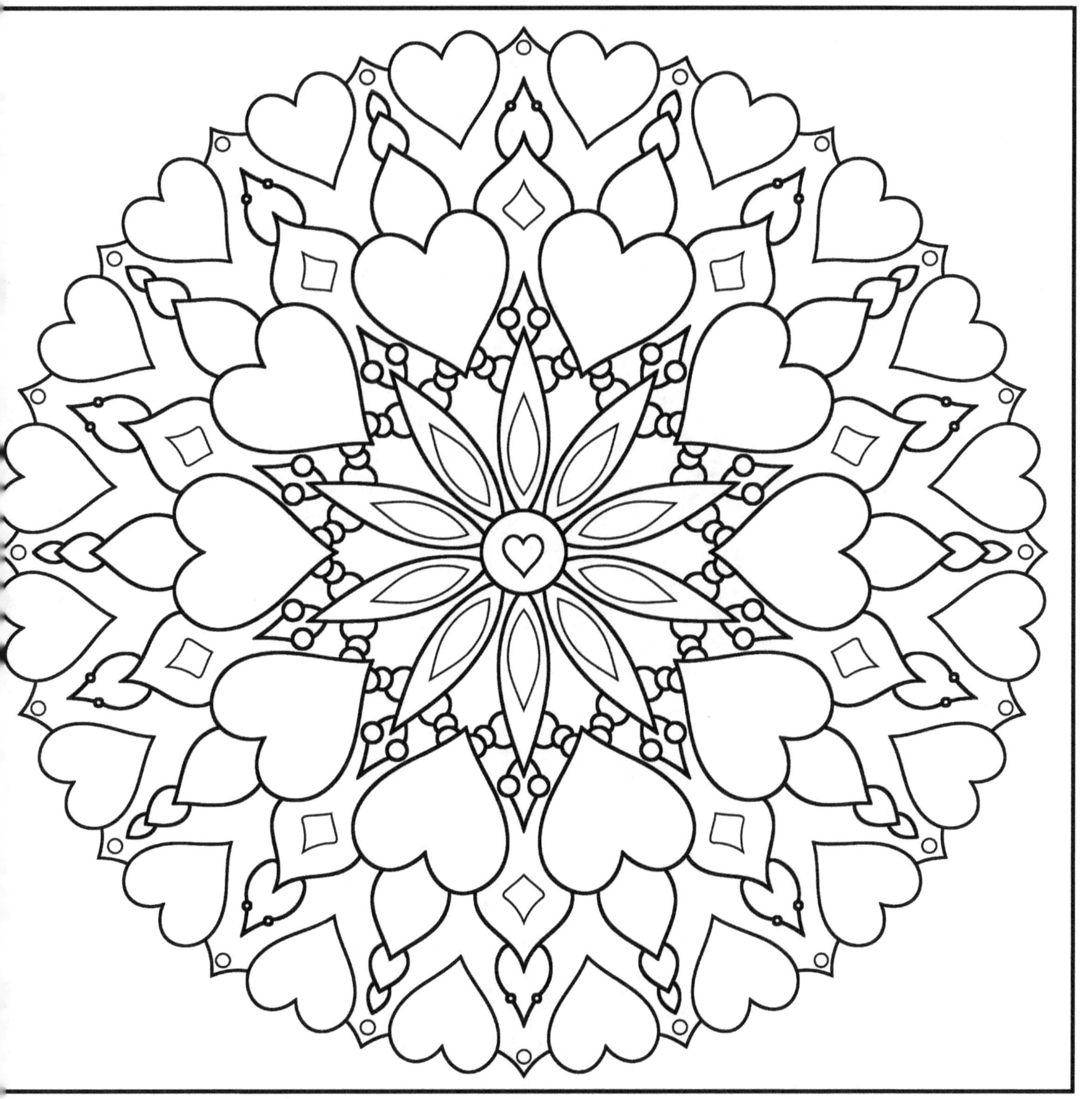

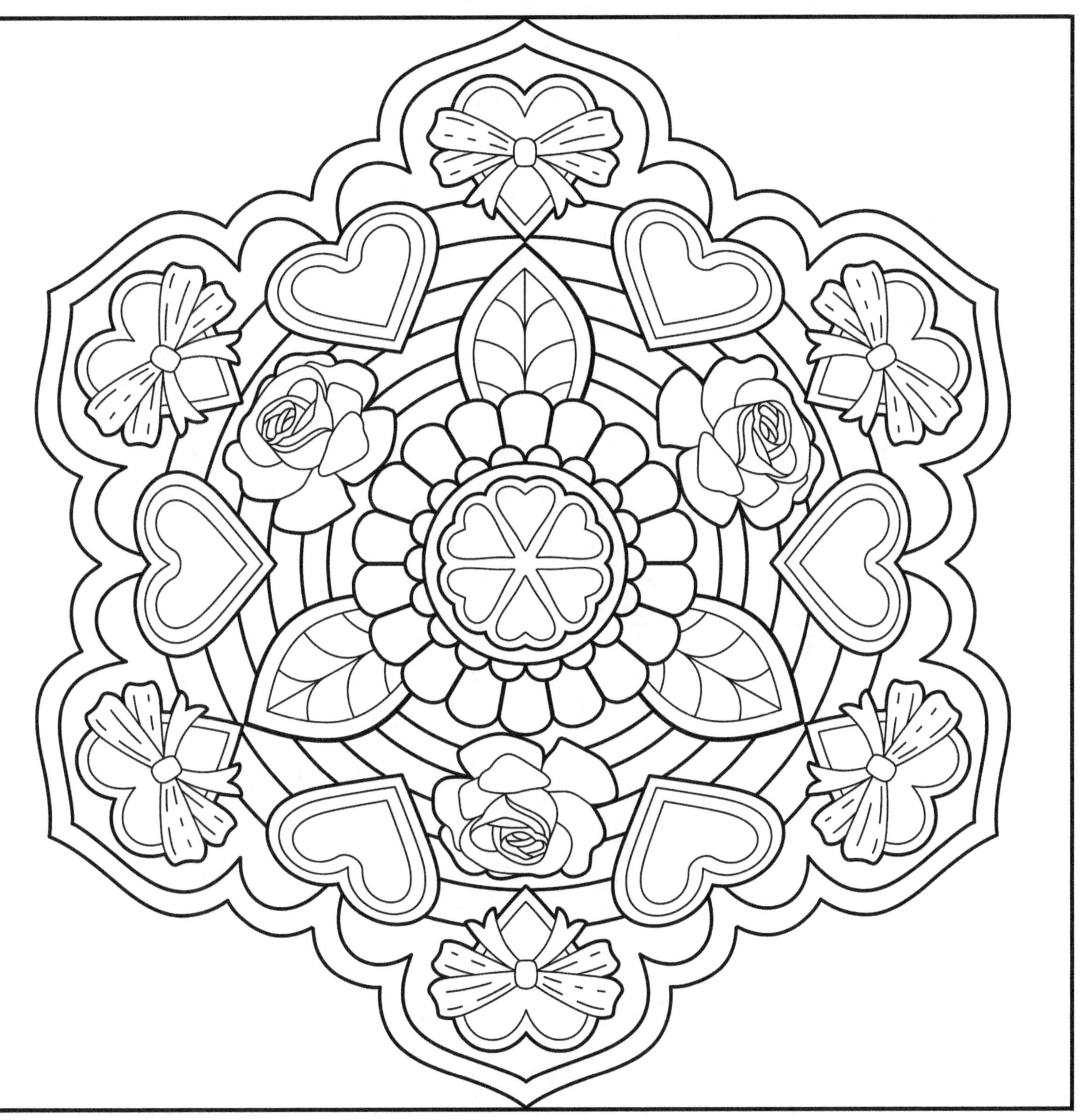

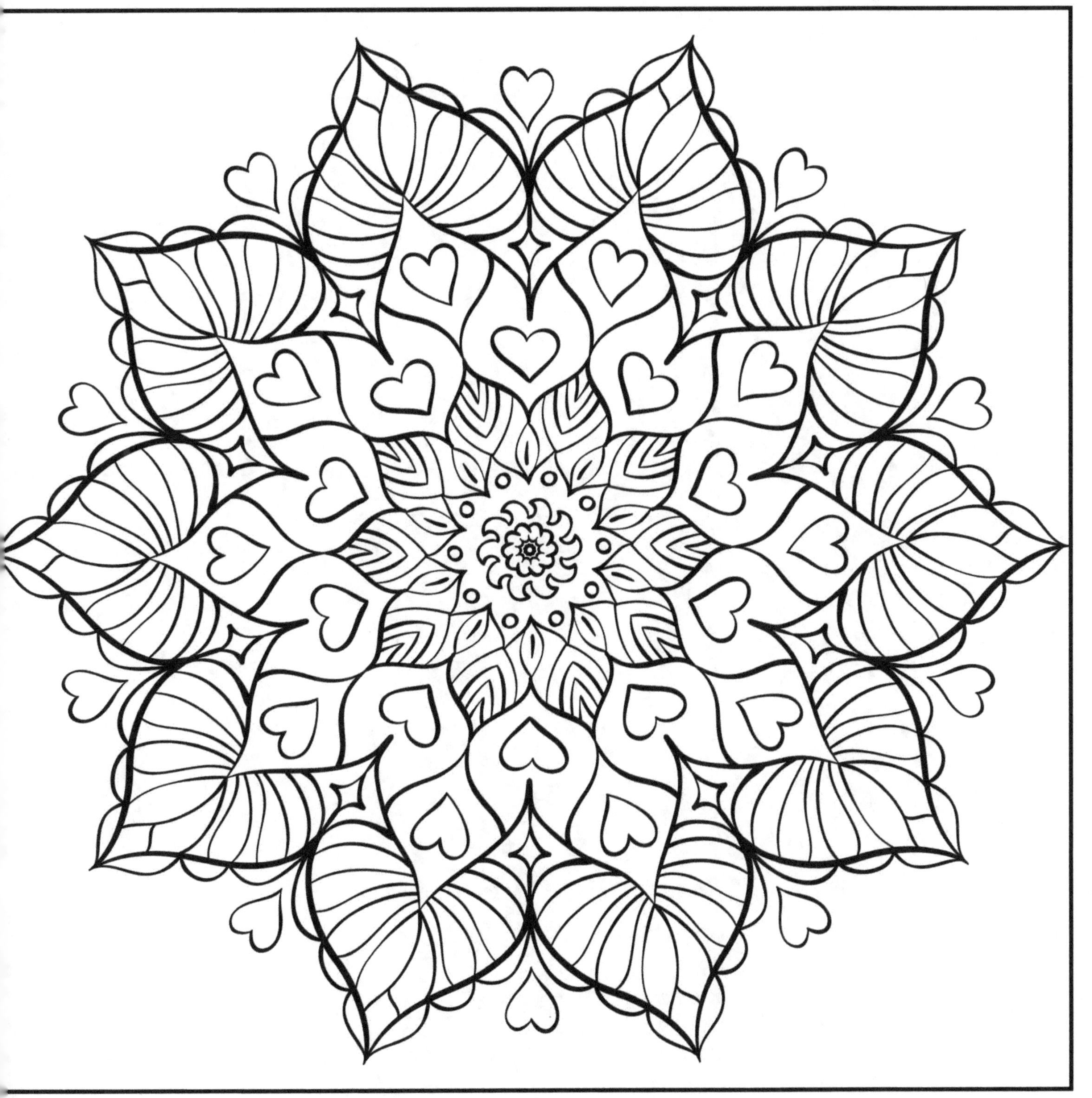

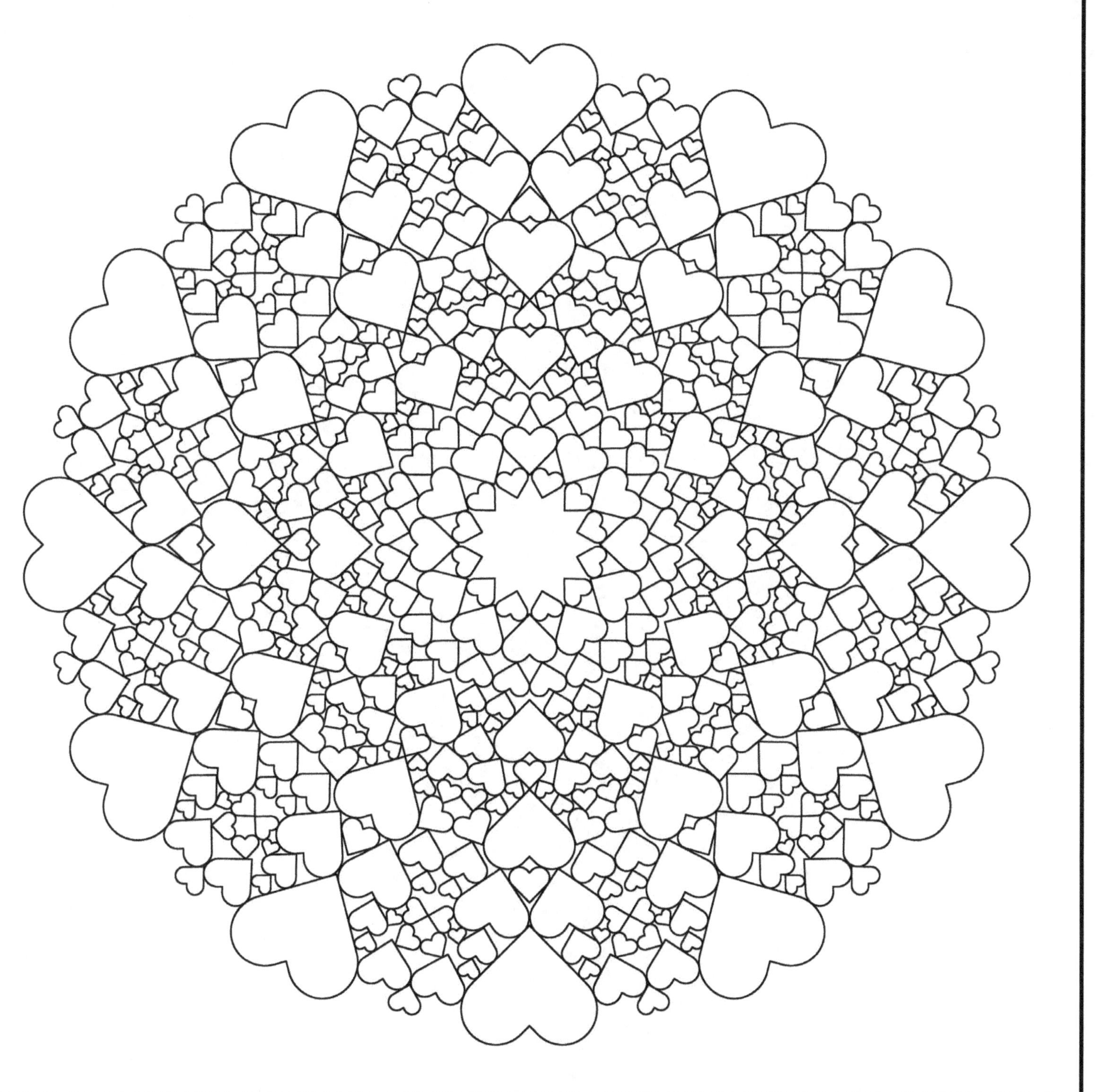

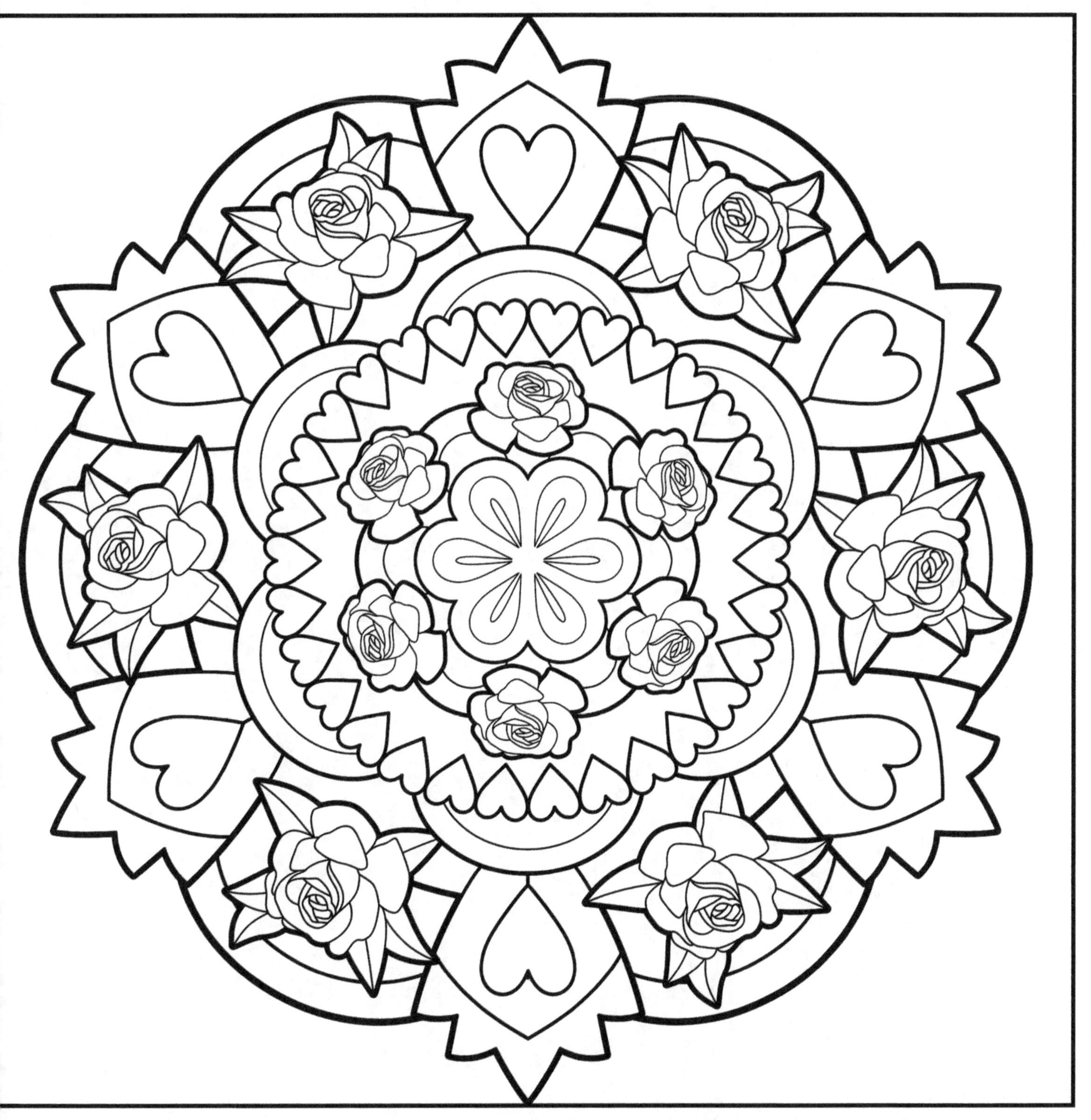

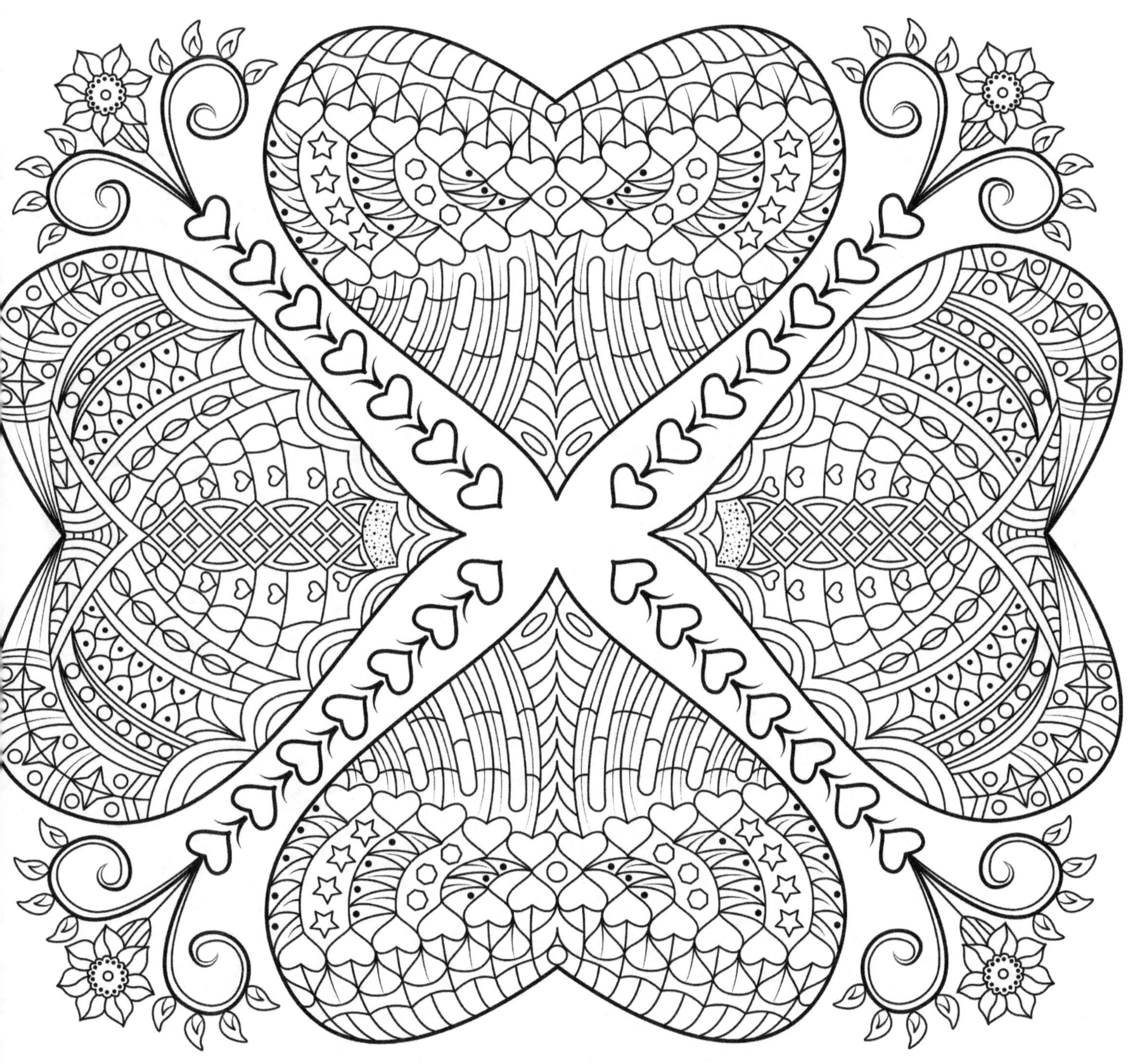

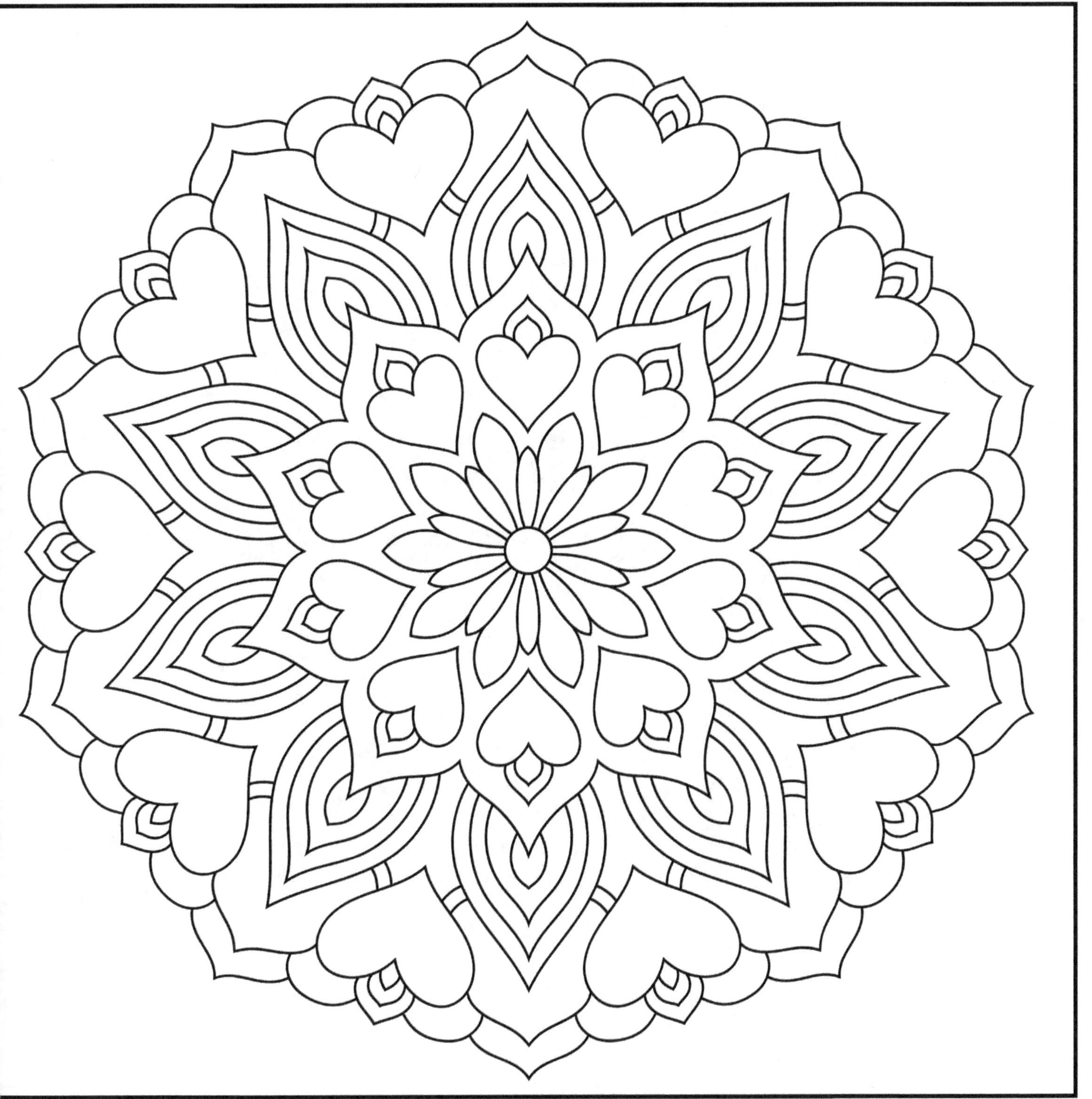

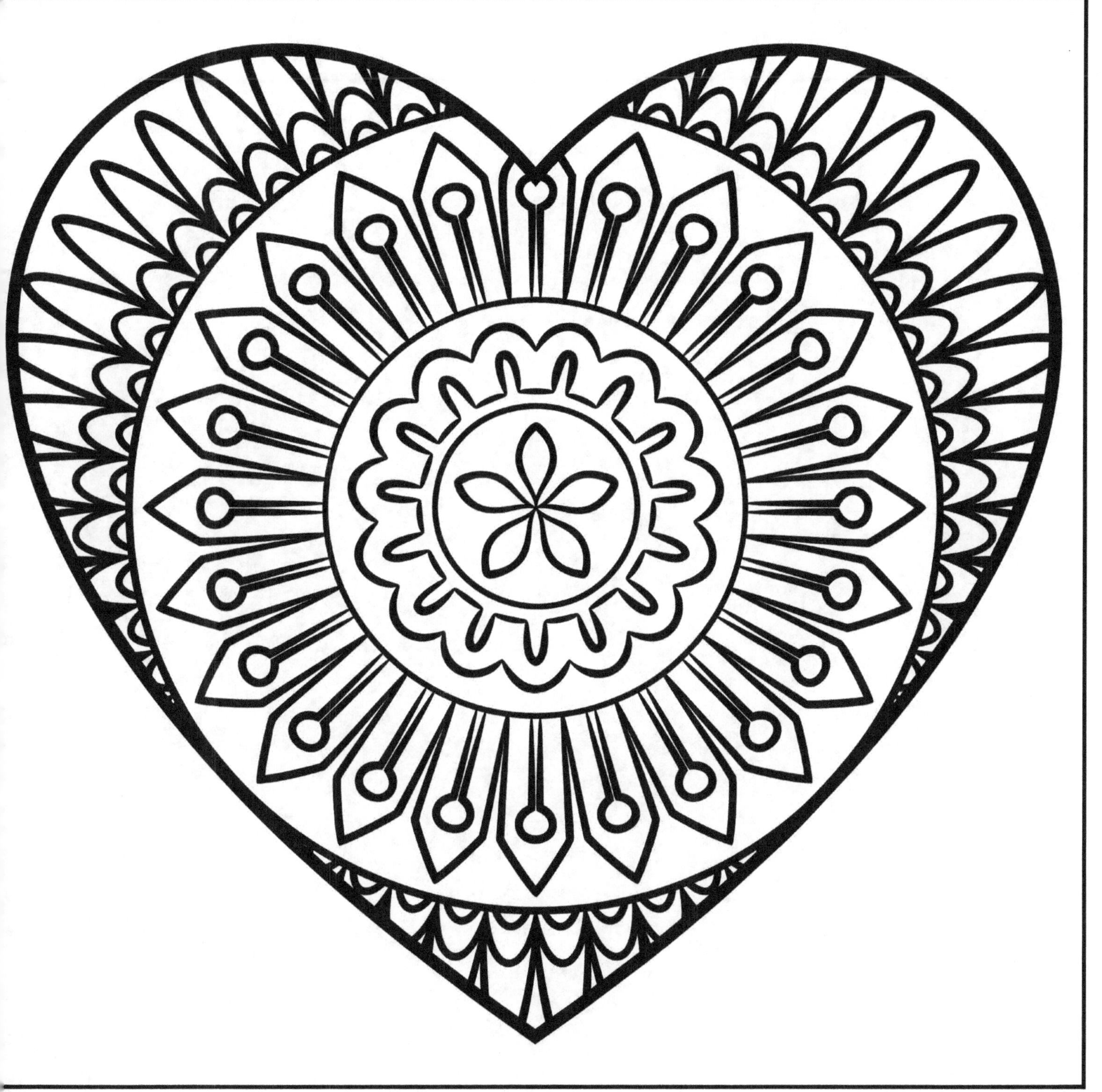

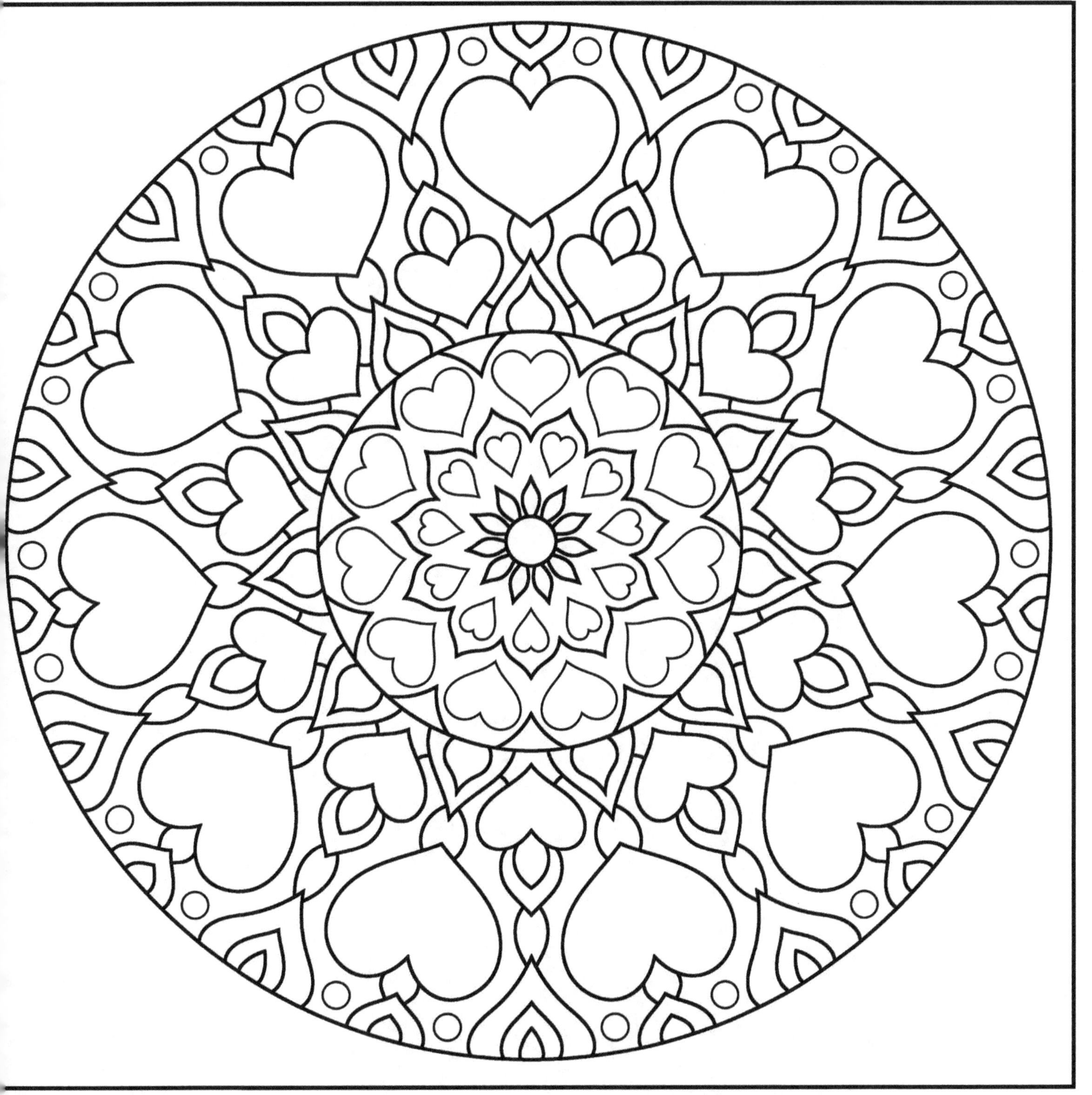

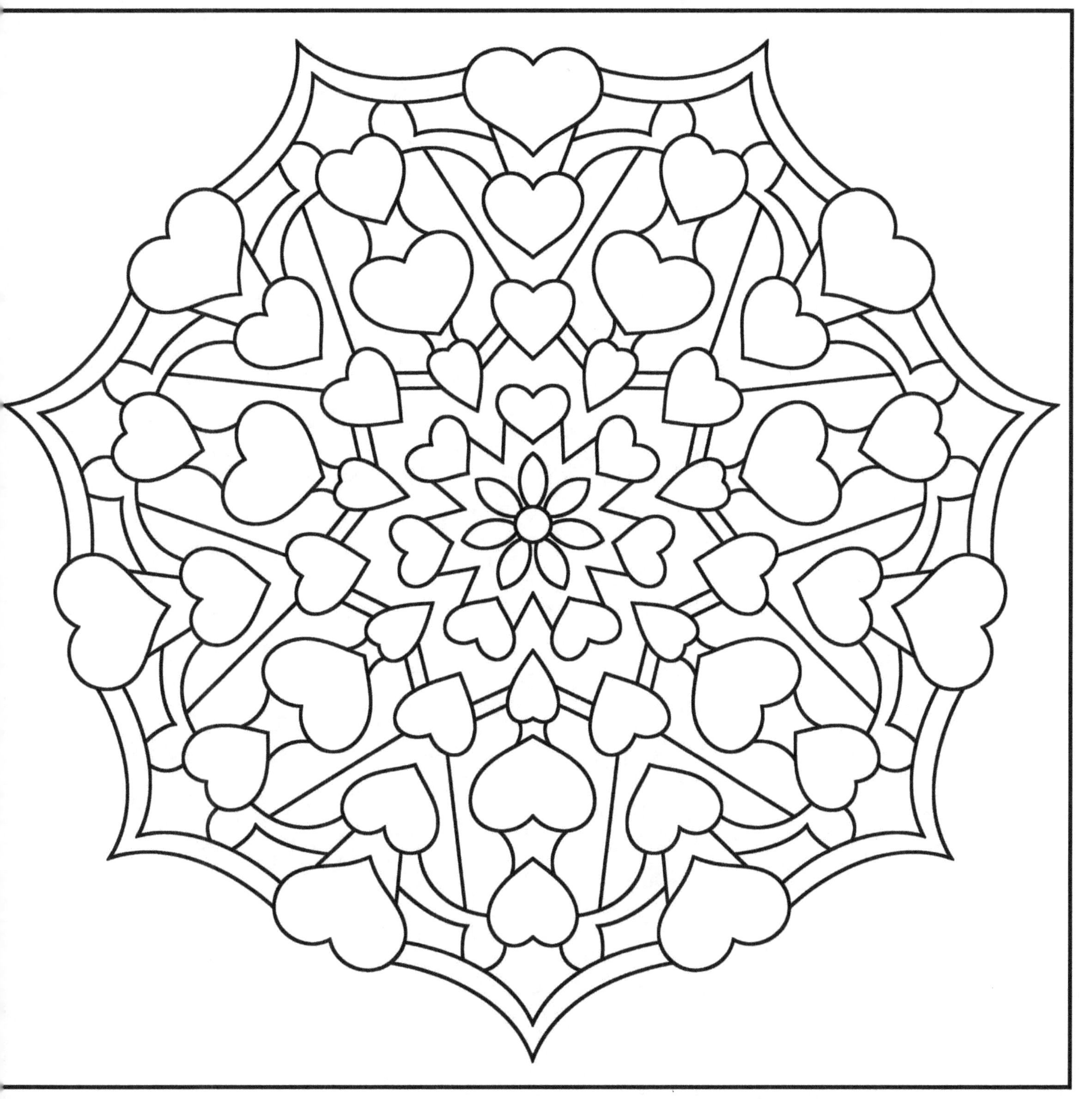

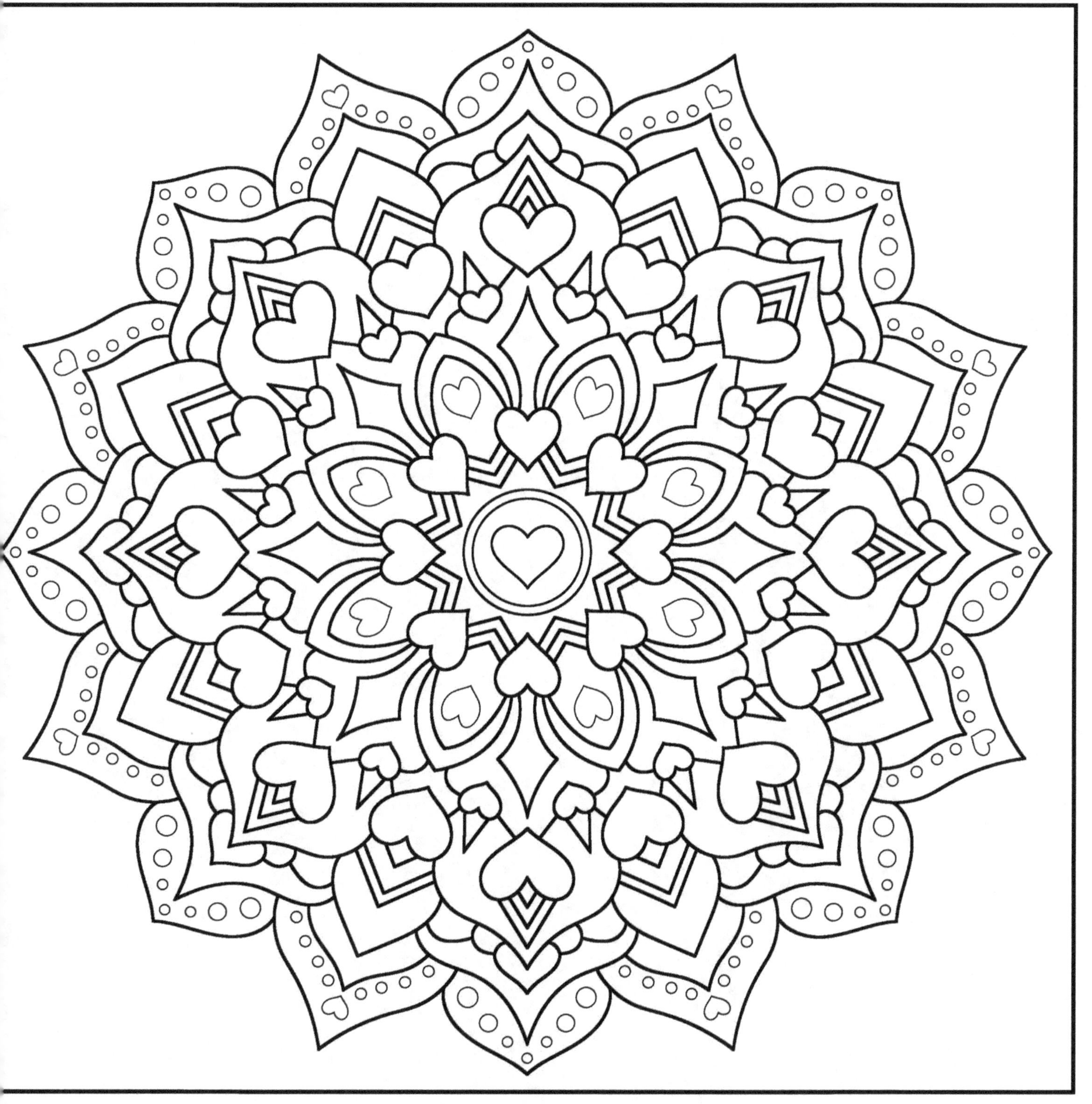

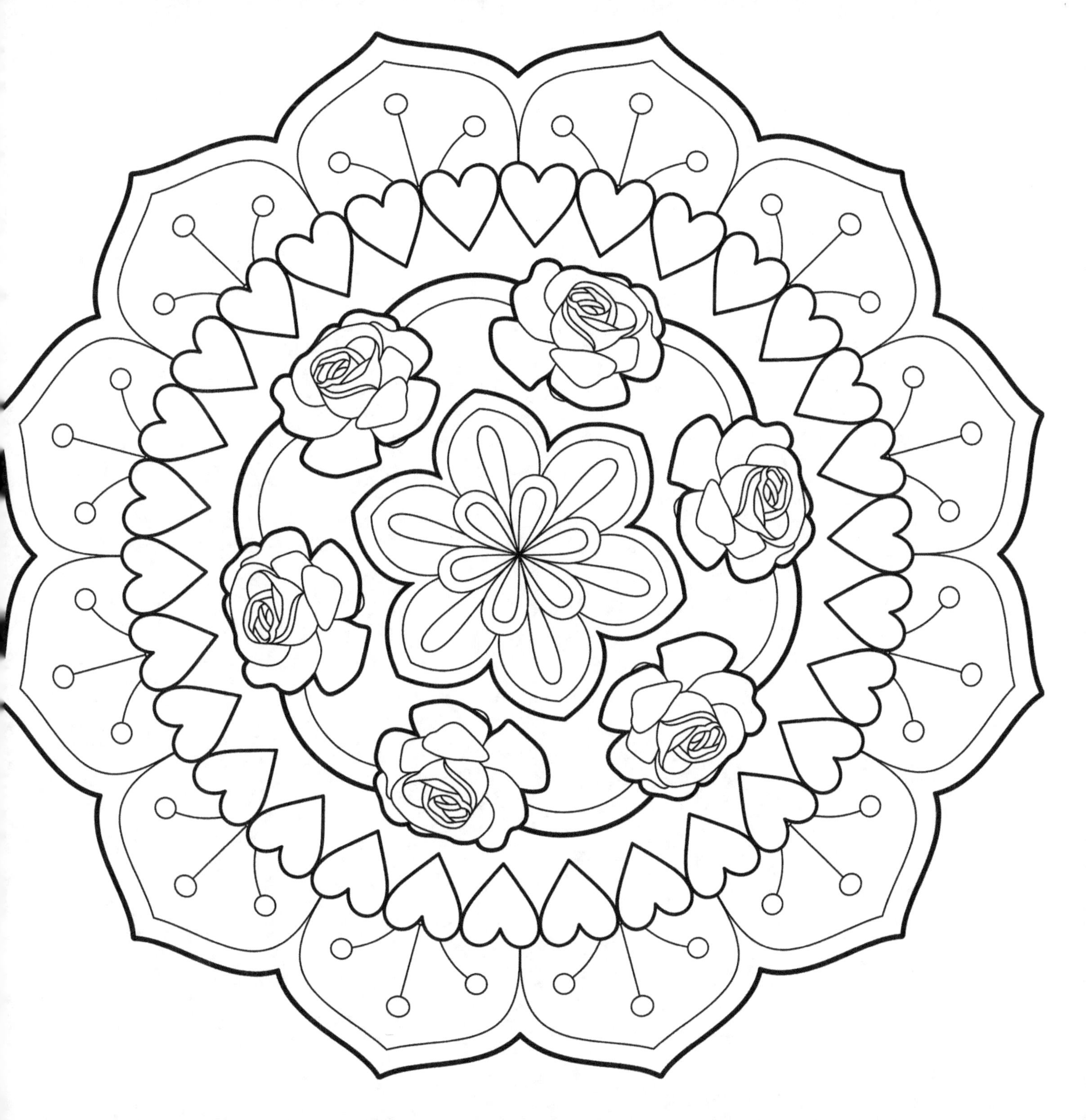

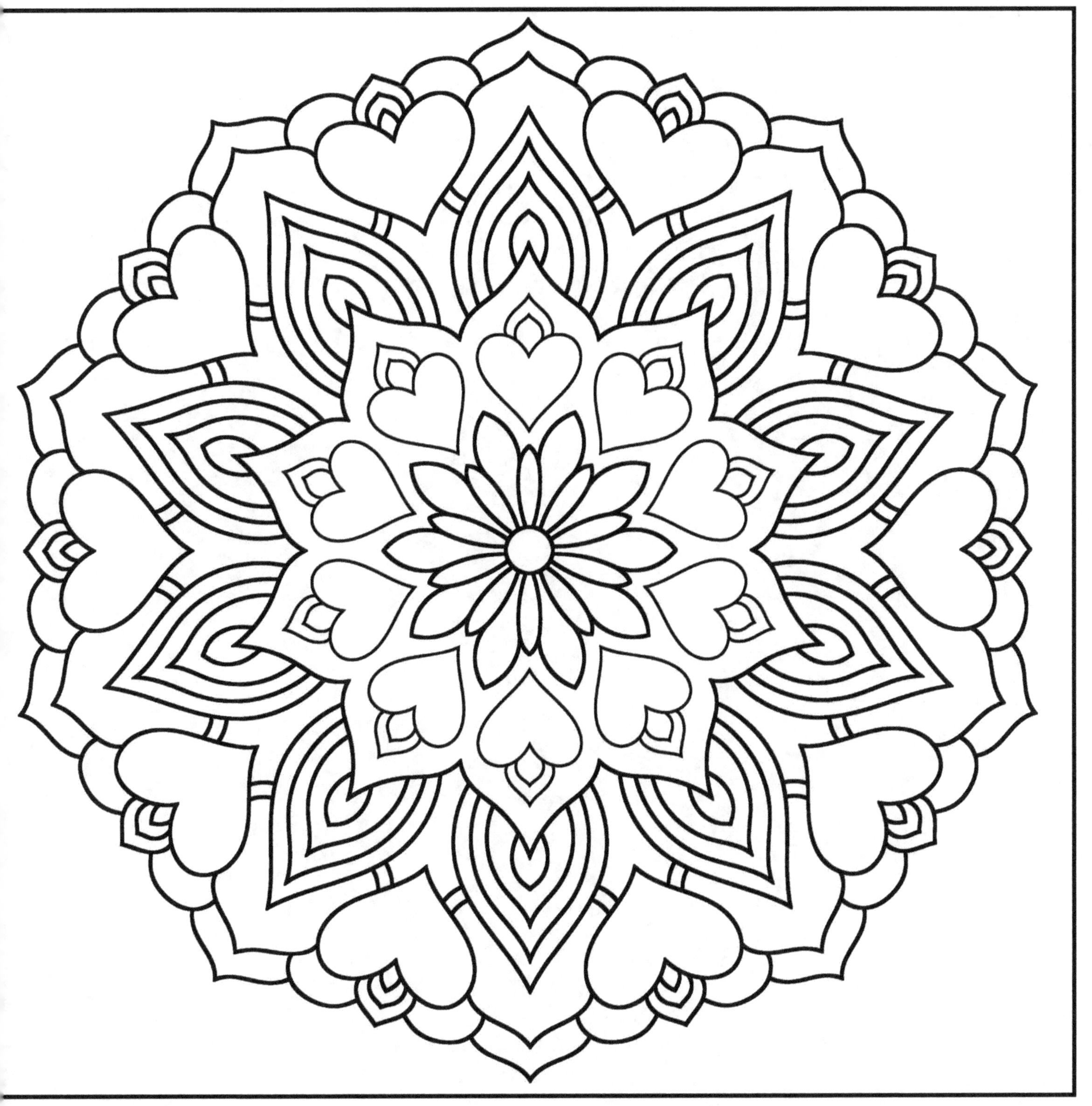

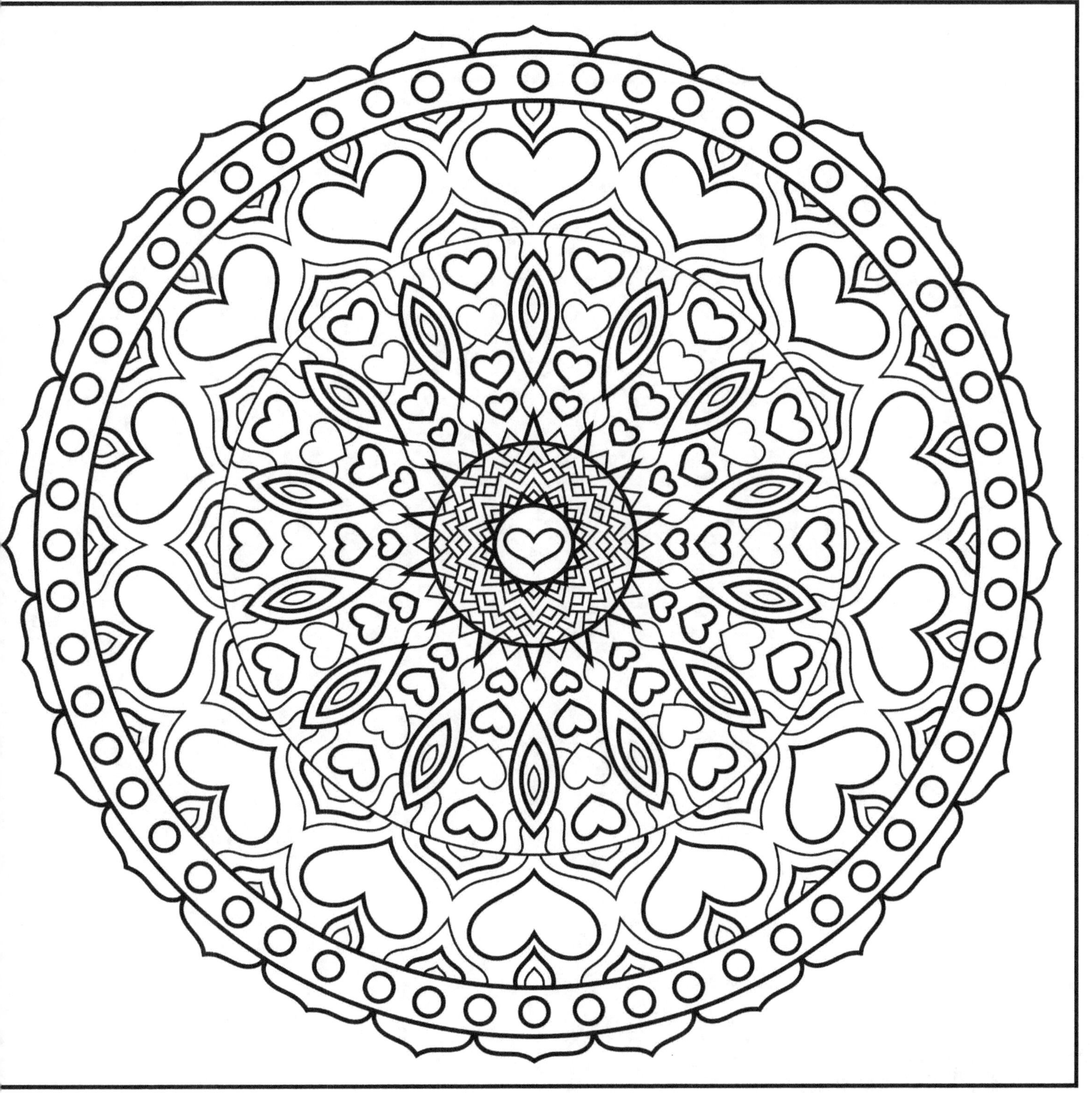